MW01697927

When Soul and Spirit Agree

Dr. Leo Natale

When Soul and Spirit Agree

BRIDGE PUBLISHING
South Plainfield, NJ

Unless otherwise indicated, the Scripture quotations in this publication are from the King James version of the Bible.

When Soul and Spirit Agree by Dr. Leo Natale
ISBN 0-88270-683-7
Library of Congress Catalog Card Number Pending

Published by:
Bridge Publishing
2500 Hamilton Blvd.
South Plainfield, NJ 07080

Printed in the United States of America.

To my family: Carolyn, my wife; Frank, my son; and Angel, my daughter. My family has been my greatest encouragement. They were always there for me. Every time I would receive an illumination from the Holy Spirit, I would bombard them to get their approval or witness. They never got tired or bored with my rambling on and on.

My wife is my greatest critic, exhorter, and friend. She constantly encouraged me to write this book. I never felt that I could, but through her faithful edification, I was able to do it. I thank God for my wife. The Bible says, "He who finds a wife finds a good thing, and obtains favor from the Lord" (Prov. 18:22, NKJV).

Contents

Preface ix

1. The Session 1
2. The Concept of Man 7
3. Two Kinds of Wisdom 29
4. The Heart of Man 37
5. Man—An Intelligent Being with a Free Will 53
6. Spirit, Soul, and Body 61
7. Active Faith and How It Works 81
8. The Word—The Vehicle of God 101

Preface

> Then God said, "Let Us make man in Our image, according to Our likeness; let them have dominion over the fish of the sea, and over the birds of the air, and over the cattle, over all the earth and over every creeping thing that creeps on the earth" (Gen. 1:26 NKJV).

People know how to devise methods to mine silver and refine gold, to dig iron from the earth, and to process the earth's minerals in many facets which will benefit humanity. People know how to put light into darkness so that a mine shaft can be sunk deep into the earth to explore the earth, and to find sapphires and gold dust, and treasures that no one has seen before. People know how to tear apart flinty rocks and how to overturn the roots of mountains. People know how to drill tunnels in the rocks and lay bare precious stones, to dam up streams of water and pan gold. These are all good. They benefit mankind and are necessary to live in this world, but this is *man's knowledge.* The purpose of this book is to provide you with a better understanding of the spiritual state of the born-again believer, and to help you bring forth this condition in the physical realm, elevating you to the next level in the completion of your spirit, soul, and body.

1

The Session

Jane, a thin, sophisticated, well-groomed young lady, was sitting across from the counselor. Her deeply set black eyes mirrored a deep excruciating pain that clearly emanated from the innermost part of her soul. She avoided direct eye contact with the counselor because she was afraid that he would discover her pain, and this would make her very uncomfortable. She always took great pride in the fact that she was in control. Her physical appearance always gave the impression that everything was fine. She was impeccably groomed, fastidiously polite, and emotionally composed.

Dr. Brian, a distinguished, well-built, athletic man in his late forties, nodded politely and began to make conversation with her. His first impression was, "What is she doing here?" As the conversation continued, Dr. Brian began to observe his patient. Her eyes showed that her soul was tormented and anguished. He realized she was a time bomb that was ready to explode.

Dr. Brian perceived that Jane was trying to conceal her true feelings. She was frazzled to the point of exhaustion, but she continued to put on the appearance of a self-assured person who was in control.

Dr. Brian smoothly and soothingly continued to converse with Jane. He complimented her on her appearance and composure, and asked her if he could be of any assistance. She casually began to make excuses by saying that she really did not need any help, she just needed direction. Dr. Brian asked her if there was any particular area of her life in which she needed direction. She replied very vaguely, "I guess I just need general direction for my life." Jane was avoiding the real issue, and the doctor knew it. He didn't want to frighten her or cause her to become stifled, however, so he nodded his head in agreement with her request.

The emaciated, frazzled young lady, who displayed erratic and neurotic tendencies that were covered by a false appearance of confidence, now became relaxed and secure. It appeared that she felt she was ready to trust her counselor. She knew that the doctor was aware of what she was doing, but he wasn't placing any demands on her. He wasn't pressuring her, but was giving her the liberty of uncovering her torments and pains, at her own discretion.

For the first time in her life, Jane felt a complete release throughout her whole body. Every fiber of her anatomy had begun to relax. She sighed and inhaled a deep breath of air. She felt a sense of exhilaration from the very bottom of her feet to the top of her head. Simultaneously, she began to experience a clean, refreshing wave of peace filtering throughout her entire being.

She had never experienced such a feeling of peace. She had always been fearful of expressing herself because she didn't know how or where to begin. She had spent her entire life seeking the approval of others; so much so, in fact, that she lost her identity in the process. She became what others wanted her to be. She was always giving and never receiving. Her life was one of extremes. Her emotions would go from one extreme to the other with little warning. Now her life was so stressed-out that she had wanted to end it all. ("Thank God for the peace I feel now," she expressed inwardly.)

Jane earnestly desired answers to the plaguing problems that were engulfing her and the environment around her. She wanted realistic and practical solutions. She felt a need to anchor herself to a secure base. In the past, she had been tied to goals, aspirations, people, positions, and material possessions. But they all failed her. Whenever each one failed, she became more and more despondent.

Jane had been to therapy before and it had helped her immensely. The therapy did not have a lasting effect in her life, however. She found herself going to therapists on a regular basis, and had become completely dependent on them. Ultimately, however, it was to no avail; for when the therapists were not around, discouragement would set in, and she would sink deeper and deeper into depression. Her life had become like a confusing maze. There were so many loose ends, and she felt unable to tie them together because she did not know where to begin. Jane was recommended to Dr. Brian by a friend. She told Jane that this therapist was different, and she was confident that Dr. Brian would be able to help her. Jane was soon to discover what the difference was when Dr. Brian began to explain to her who he was, and how he conducted his profession. He told Jane that he was a Spirit-filled, born-again Christian, who anchored his life to the Word of God.

When Jane heard this, she displayed an outburst of excitement. Actually, she could not truly understand her feeling of exhilaration to any particular action, but presumed it had something to do with a word the doctor used, "anchored." Jane had been a Christian for many years and she attended church regularly. She practiced all of her beliefs faithfully, but she never pictured herself as being anchored to the Word of God. She always thought that she had to be anchored to someone or something tangible. She asked Dr. Brian to explain to her what he meant by being anchored to the Word.

The therapist began his interpretation by quoting Romans 12:2,

> And be not conformed to this world: but be ye transformed by the renewing of your mind, that ye may prove what is that good, and acceptable, and perfect, will of God.

He went on to explain that man was created by God and for God. Man had been anchored to God from the very beginning. He then was separated from God by sin, but was restored again through the redemptive sacrifice of Jesus at Calvary. Jesus and the Word are one and the same (John 1:1), and when we anchor ourselves to the Word, we are joined to Christ.

"The Word is power, and it will transform you into

the image and likeness of your Creator," he pointed out. Jane's exhausted and depleted soul began to absorb what Dr. Brian was saying, and new life began to flow into her. She felt a release within herself, experiencing a freedom she never had before. For the first time in her life, she strongly believed that she would receive all of the answers she needed.

Dr. Brian began to sense that something wonderful was happening to Jane. She was responding, and he was now ready to explain his concept of man . . . .

2

The Concept of Man

In order to understand mankind, you must understand the makeup of people. Man is a spirit-being and he has a soul. His spirit and soul are not visible to the human eye. The spirit of man and his soul abide in a human, physical body. Spirit, soul, and body comprise the complete makeup of man. In First Thessalonians 5:23 we read, "And the very God of peace sanctify you wholly; and I pray God your whole spirit and soul and body be preserved blameless unto the coming of our Lord Jesus Christ."

The spirit of man is his being, and this is the part of man that is created in the image and likeness of God (Gen. 1:26). The breath of life is in the spirit of man. In Genesis 2:7, we read how God formed man's body from the elements of the earth, and put man's spirit into his body and it became a living being.

In the Gospel of John, Jesus states, "God is a Spirit: and they that worship him must worship him in spirit and in truth" (John 4:24). Jesus is making a very profound statement to the woman of Samaria in this passage. He is literally declaring that man is a spirit-being like God. Who would be better able to make this declaration than Jesus? It was by Him and for Him that God (*Elohim*) man was created (Col. 1:16).

The spirit of man operating in a physical body was now able to relate to the physical realm through the body. His spirit quickened the material body and gave it life, and through this action he would now be able to be present in two realms—the spiritual (the unseen) and the physical (that which is seen).

Man is God's masterpiece and God made him to be the master of all the earth and everything in it. Man was now able to perform great spiritual feats in his physical form. Some examples of this phenomenon can be seen in Adam, the first man created by God; and in Jesus, who was the last Adam (1 Cor. 15:45). One of the supernatural feats that Adam demonstrated is recorded in Genesis 2:20, where it states that he named all of the cattle, the fowl of the air, and the beasts of the field. God created them and He gave Adam the responsibility of naming them all. God was demonstrating the position and authority He gave to man.

Jesus is the perfect example of the new-creation man. He displayed His natural abilities at will in His everyday living. Jesus was able to do this because He was operating from the spiritual realm. In the spiritual realm, there is no lack. (See Eph. 1:3 and 2 Cor. 4:18.) Jesus saw all the provisions as being already manifested. In the Gospel of Matthew, verses 14:14-21, Jesus displayed the authority given Him. This is the account of the feeding of the multitudes. The apostles brought Him five small loaves of bread and two fishes. There were over 5,000 men, plus an unknown number of women and children, and they were all fed to the full because Jesus had the authority to perform miracles. The Bible records that there were twelve baskets full of leftovers.

When the basket of bread and fishes was brought to Jesus, He prayed and blessed them and told the apostles to distribute them to the people. As the people took from the basket, it kept replenishing itself. They were dipping right into the spiritual realm and bringing it forth into the physical realm. This was a supernatural act that was accomplished by a man because of the authority of God. Jesus was operating in His God-given authority *as a man under covenant.*

The Bible tells of another time when God fed His people in the everyday, practical sense. God sent quail to the children of Israel (Num. 11:31). There were so many quail that the Israelites were standing four feet high in them. One translation of the Bible states that the smallest amount of food anyone gathered was 100 bushels of quail. The *God of Abundant Living* was at work, supplying the needs of His people, and giving them more than enough.

In the Old Testament there were no born-again believers because Jesus had not yet come. God had to work things out purely in the physical realm. He spoke through the prophets as His Spirit fell upon them (Ezek. 11:5). The prophets were anointed with the Holy Spirit for a particular event or time. God could not operate from within them because they were spiritually dead. They were saved by their faith in the coming of Christ, but the physical manifestation was not yet evident. It would become manifested with the birth, death, and resurrection of Jesus Christ. Jesus would restore to man what Adam had away.

God's Word is spirit and truth. He gave us His Word in Genesis 3:15 that He would send a Redeemer, and the power of that Word was operative by faith until the coming of Jesus Christ. God's Word is spirit and truth, and His Word established in our hearts, spoken with our tongue (with the breath of life), will cut through the physical and produce the results God desires.

Hebrews 4:12 states,

> For the word of God is quick, and powerful, and sharper than any two-edged sword, piercing even to the dividing asunder of soul and spirit, and of the joints and marrow, and is a discerner of the thoughts and intents of the heart.

In Isaiah 55:11, we read,

> So shall my word be that goeth forth out of my mouth: it shall not return unto me void, but it shall accomplish that which I please, and it shall prosper in the thing whereto I sent it.

The action of the Word is spiritual and cannot be seen with physical eyes, but can be seen with spiritual eyes (2 Kings 6:17).

In Mark 4:37-41, and Luke 8:23-24, we have the account of the violent storm at sea with the apostles and Jesus in the boat. We read that Jesus was asleep, and the apostles frantically came and awakened Him. He got up and commanded the wind and sea to be calm. He commanded the atmosphere and it obeyed Him. Jesus was operating according to the principle of authority first outlined in Genesis 1:26. Man was given all authority and power to rule over all of this earth.

> Then God said, "Let Us make man in Our image, according to Our likeness; let them have dominion over the fish of the sea, and over the birds of the air, and over the cattle, over all the earth and over every creeping thing that creeps on the earth" (Gen. 1:26 NKJV).

God created man in His image and after His likeness. This means that we can be like Him. He is our Father, and children should act like their Father. Jesus was operating in a principle that was established on this earth by God. He was operating naturally because this was the original nature of man. To us, this feat may seem supernatural because we still have not grasped the concept of Genesis 1:26.

Regenerated man has the power and authority to do what God does on this earth. He is in command of all the earth and all that is in it because God has given him this authority. God cannot and will not violate His Word. He will stand by His Word, but man must take and use the authority that was given to him.

Adam violated this authority in Genesis 3:6 through his disobedience, and he lost the right to use it. But Jesus restored man to his original position through His obedience in His sacrifice on the cross and His resurrection. Mark 16:15-18 and Matthew 28:18-20 sum up what Jesus did. He became the atoning sacrifice for our sinful nature, and the complete substitute for us. He went to hell on our behalf, and was literally born-again from the bowels of hell by the power of the Holy Spirit. He then took back the authority of man from the devil and gave man's rightful spiritual authority back to him. He has taken His position in heaven for the time being and resumed the full glory of His Deity again.

Today, man is the only power on this earth. God and Satan influence him, but they do not exercise power here. Both have to work through men. Man's authority and power can operate either in the positive or the negative, depending upon their source. God is positive and Satan is negative, and the influence of one or the other will be exerted. We are affected by thoughts, and the thoughts we receive will eventually be expressed through words. "Death and life are in the power of the tongue; and they that love it shall eat the fruit thereof" (Prov. 18:21).

Let's take a closer look at Proverbs 18:21. Notice that the first word of the verse is "death." I always quoted this Scripture as "Life and death are in the power of the tongue." I was amazed when I realized that the word "death" was first.

I know the character of God. He is a positive being, and I could not understand why He would put death first. But then I realized that the verse was dealing with the mind of man and man's first instinct is to speak negatively. Negativism is death. This is why the Bible states that we must renew our minds to the Word of God so that we will speak life instead of death. As Romans 12:2 states, ". . . be ye transformed by the renewing of your mind . . . ."

Notice also in Proverbs 18:21 that death and life are called power, and that power is *in the tongue.* Three important things must be recognized here. First, there is *death,* and death is negative and destructive—its author is Satan.

Second, there is *life,* and life is positive, good and fulfilling. All good things come from God. Philippians 4:8 states,

> Finally brethren, whatsoever things are true, whatsoever things are honest, whatsoever things are just, whatsoever things are pure, whatsoever things are lovely, whatsoever things are of good report; if there be any virtue, and if there be any praise, think on these things.

James 1:17 states,

> Every good gift and every perfect gift is from above, and cometh down from the Father of Lights, with whom is no variableness, neither shadow of turning.

Third, there is *power* and power is in the tongue. The tongue is the vehicle that will bring forth the power of good or evil. In this universe, it is the spoken Word of God that has power. In every instance from the very beginning, God spoke His Word. This power of *speaking* was given to man. (See Gen. 2:23.) He was acting in the likeness of God. But unfortunately man became corrupt and instead of speaking like God, he began to speak like the devil. At one point in time, God had to come down and confuse man's language because humanity was destroying itself through pride (Gen. 11:7). There is a good source, which is God, and there is an evil source, which is the devil. In order for either of these sources to operate on this earth, they must operate through man.

Man is responsible for his destiny. He can have whatever he commits himself to. He can have life (the Word) and flourish, or he can have death (the world's wisdom) and only exist. Proverbs 18:21 warns, ". . . and they that love it shall eat the fruit thereof." This simply means that whatever you partake of is what you will receive. You can feast on the Word and be blessed, or you can feed on the world's wisdom and struggle.

Animals cannot bear spiritual fruit, but human beings can. Jesus talks about this in John 15:5. Jesus calls himself the vine, and we are the branches. He says that if we abide in Him, we (the branches) will bear much fruit. Abiding in Him means to abide in the Word. Man is the fruit-bearer (branches), and Christ is the vine. This verse is a perfect example of man allowing God (the good source) to operate through him.

Man is a spirit-being and he has a soul. What is the soul? The Hebrew word for soul is *nephesh,* and its Greek counterpart is *psuche.* The soul of man is defined as that which contains the faculties of thought, action, and emotion. The soul produces man's feelings. The spirit is man's principle of life. Both the spirit and soul are unseen by the natural eye. The spirit and soul give life to the body. The body is only the vessel or the receiver of what the spirit and soul produce.

In the beginning when God created man, his soul was part of his spirit. Soul and spirit operated in complete unity and in one accord. Man and God were so linked together that the glory of God shown in and around Adam and Eve. Man was clothed with God's glory.

Genesis 2:25 reveals, "And they were both naked, the man and his wife, and were not ashamed." Man was created to live in this perfection forever. He would never grow old because his body was constantly living out the perfection of the spirit within. He was ageless, just like God.

In Genesis 2:17, God tells Adam, "But of the tree of the knowledge of good and evil, thou shalt not eat of it: for in the day that thou eatest thereof thou shalt surely die." God had to tell Adam and Eve about this tree because He wanted them to know that evil was already on the earth in the presence of the devil. He is the epitome and essence of evil. Evil began with him, and was with him, and he was here on this earth (Isa. 14:12-15; Ezek. 28:12-19). Jesus said, ". . . I beheld Satan as lightning fall from heaven" (Luke 10:18). Jesus was there at the beginning when Satan fell.

God's nature is good, and this goodness operated through His created being, Adam. This goodness overcame all evil and provided all the answers. God foreknew that Satan would be coming around, so He warned Adam and Eve. But the devil is cunning and he tricked Eve (Gen. 3:13). When Satan asked Eve about the tree, she answered him in the way God told her,

> . . . We may eat of the fruit of the trees of the garden: But of the fruit of the tree which is in the midst of the garden, God hath said, Ye shall not eat of it, neither shall ye touch it, lest ye die (Gen. 3:2-3).

Then Satan answered her and said, in effect, "You won't die when you eat the fruit of that tree. Your eyes will be open and then you will be as gods knowing good from evil" (Gen. 3:4-5). The devil lied to Eve. Adam and Eve were already gods on the earth. Psalms 82:6 explicitly says, "I have said, Ye are gods; and all of you are children of the most High."

Satan was trying to appeal to Eve through her senses. In Genesis 3:6, we see that the woman saw the tree as good for food (lust of the flesh), and that it was pleasant for the eyes (lust of the eyes), and a tree to be desired to make one wise (pride of life). Satan was able, through his deceptiveness, to get Eve's attention through her physical nature. She forgot who she was, and desired something that God hadn't given her. She already had God's intelligence, and God's supernatural ability (knowledge of good). What she didn't have was the knowledge of evil, which is of the devil.

Satan was able to draw Eve's attention away from what she had, and focus it on what she did not have. Because he is the master deceiver, he made it look very appealing, and much desired. How did he do this? He told her, "ye shall be as gods, knowing good and evil" (Gen. 3:5). Good *and* evil. She already knew good, but she didn't know evil. Now Satan had Eve's attention, and he began to paint a picture of what he wanted her to see. This is evident in Genesis 3:6, where she saw that the tree was good for food, pleasant to the eyes, and would make one wise.

Eve was no longer acting from a spiritual sense, but from a purely carnal motive. She was moved by her emotions. She was operating from the soul-oriented area of her spiritual being. She had conceived sin in her soul by receiving the suggestions or thoughts of the devil—

and she gave life to these by her act of disobedience when she ate the fruit.

Then when she gave the fruit to Adam and he ate it, they died spiritually. They became separated from God. Up until that time, their sense realm had been totally synchronized with God. Now they were on their own because they had listened to the devil. He became their source of information from then until the death they would eventually experience in their bodies.

I would like to make something very clear here. The soul is not a separate entity within the body. Man is the only entity, and he is called *spirit.* The spirit-man has a soul, and the soul and spirit abide in the body. The soul and the spirit are what the Bible calls the "inner man." The inner man operates through a physical body. The inner man is spiritual and cannot be seen by the natural eye. The body, on the other hand, is physical, and can be seen. The unseen, in effect, operates through the seen.

Restoration for man (man's spirit) was immediately provided for by God in Genesis 3:15 through His promise of a Redeemer. Although the promise would not be physically manifested until the coming of Jesus, the power and authority of the promise were immediately in effect when God spoke. Jesus became the propitiation for man's sin in the spirit realm, and would manifest this in the physical realm through his birth, death and resurrection. Because of what Jesus did, man—including Old Testament man—could now become a new creation. A *new* creation comes through the application of faith. "Now faith is the substance of things hoped for, the evidence of things not seen" (Heb. 11:1). The new creation is accomplished solely by God. It is a gift from

Him. We do nothing but receive it through an act of our wills (Rom. 10:9-10).

Because the soul part of man sinned, it was necessary to restore his soul to its originally created status. Isaiah 53:10 states,

> Yet it pleased the Lord to bruise him; he hath put him to grief: when thou shalt make his soul an offering for sin, he shall see his seed, he shall prolong his days, and the pleasure of the Lord shall prosper in his hand.

Note the reference to the soul: "thou shalt make His soul as an offering for sin." The word "soul" in the Hebrew is *nephesh,* which means the area of man that is the center of his intelligence, emotions and will. *It is not the spirit of man.* The Hebrew word for spirit is *ruwachy* for the spirit of God; or *neshamah* for the spirit of man.

Our Scripture verse definitely implies that God would make the *soul* of Jesus become a sin offering for our soul. Just as the blood of Jesus was the Atonement for our salvation, and the stripes on His back were for the healing of our bodies, His soul became the offering for the soul of man. Adam and Eve sinned from their sense-related parts, which are governed by the soul. Paul summed it up in First Thessalonians 5:23,

> And the very God of peace sanctify you wholly; and I pray God your whole spirit and soul and body be preserved blameless unto the coming of our Lord Jesus Christ.

The next verse tells us how it is accomplished: "Faithful is he that calleth you, who also will do it."

Jesus became the complete substitute for man.

In Matthew 26:38 and Mark 14:34, we find Jesus saying, ". . . my soul is exceeding sorrowful, even unto death . . . ." The Greek word that is used for "sorrowful" in Matthew is *lupeo,* which means to be distressed; to be sad; to be made sorrowful; also sadness, grief, grievous, grudgingly, heaviness, and sorrow. The Greek word for "sorrowful" that Mark uses is *perilupos.* It is connected with two other words, *peran* and *peri.* The word *peran* means to pierce through to the other side, and *peri* implies through, all around, all over the subject, occasion or superlative point. *Peri* is used with regard to the locality, circumstance, or general period— also about, above, against, at, on behalf of. *Perilupos* means to be grieved all around.

But in order to get a full meaning of what the Bible is saying, we have to synopsize the total meaning of the three words. Jesus' soul was being pierced through to the other side. What is "the other side?" It is the opposite side of His divine nature—the nature of man. Jesus would then do a complete makeover of man's soul. He would give us His nature as He had taken ours. This is the reason why He was so sorrowful.

In Hebrews 5:7-9 we read,

> Who in the days of His flesh, when he had offered up prayers and supplications with strong crying and tears unto him that was able to save him from death, and was heard in that he feared; Though he were a Son, yet learned he obedience by the things which he suffered; And being made perfect He became the author of eternal salvation unto all them that obey Him.

Jesus, at this time, was taking on His soul, the sin nature of man. He was experiencing the torment and anguish of man's soul. At one point, Jesus asked the Father to remove the cup that He was enduring. This torment was so intense and unbearable that He, in His flesh, could not do it. But when He gave it to the Father—"not my will, but your will be done"—He was able to be led through the task that was set before Him. Jesus endured the cross because He foresaw the joy of the resurrection that would eventually free man's soul from torment and anguish, and set the whole man free once and for all. Redeeming the complete man through the shed blood of Jesus Christ, who took the grief of man in His soul and the infirmities of man in His flesh, was God's ultimate goal from the beginning of time (Heb. 10:5-10).

The soul of man is the center of his intellect, emotions and will. The soul cannot be seen with the physical eye, but produces results that can be seen. The soul produces life emanating from the spirit of man, and brings into existence the experiences or issues of life into the physical realm. Life and experiences can be categorized as being essentially the same. To live is to experience, and to experience is to live. The Hebrew word for life and living is *nephesh. Nephesh* is also used to describe the soul, or what we would refer to as the "natural man." The Greek translation for soul is *psuche.* This is the root from which we get our word *psyche, which also means the soul or mind.*

Encompassed in the soul is the memory, and the memory of man is structured in his heart in picture form. All the information that man has in his heart comes in through his senses. Knowledge does not always have to come in through the mind by a thought. It can be received by any of the senses: sight, taste, smell, hearing, or touch. Because we inherited our nature from Adam, our senses still maintain the memory of sin. As born-again Christians, we are to be led by our spirits, and not to be influenced by the flesh or the sense realm. The only way that this can be done is to have the soul or mind renewed by the Word of God (Rom. 12:2).

Proverbs 4:23 says, "Keep thy heart with all diligence; for out of it are the issues of life." Another word for *issues* would be *experiences*. So we can say that the heart of man, which is part of his soul, is full of experiences. We are commanded to keep our heart with all diligence. We are to monitor what comes into our heart as experiences, because what we build up in our heart eventually will be acted out in life. In each and every instance where the word "life" is used in the above verses, it is translated *nephesh,* which means soul. This definitely indicates that man, through his soul, is responsible for the outcome of his actions in the physical realm—regardless of whether he is aware of it or not.

Proverbs 13:3 states, "He that keepeth his mouth keepeth his life . . . ." Proverbs 15:4 states, "A wholesome tongue is a tree of life: but perverseness therein is a breach in the spirit." Proverbs 14:30 records, "A sound heart is the life of the flesh: but envy the rottenness of the bones." Proverbs 22:4 states, "By humility and fear of the Lord are riches, and honour, and life." To reiterate, the word that is used for life is the same translation for soul, which is *nephesh.* In each of the above Scriptures, there is a reference to the physical being. These Scriptures are clearly dealing with our souls. The Bible emphatically states and teaches that we must renew and maintain our souls with the Word of God (Rom. 12:2), and the results will be life in our flesh in addition to riches and honor. By humbling ourselves before the Lord, and observing, meditating, and doing His Word, success is guaranteed in all that we endeavor (Ps. 1:1-3).

Proverbs 20:27 states, "The spirit of man is the candle of the Lord, searching all the inward parts of the belly." This is a very interesting Scripture. It is one of the few times that you will see, "the spirit of man" in the Old Testament. This word "spirit" for man, in the Hebrew-Chaldean is *neshamah* (nee-sheaw-mah). This word means, "of divine inspiration, intellect, breath of man." The word for the Spirit of God is *Ruwach,* and is translated as breath, wind, tempest, environment, supernatural intelligence. *Ruwach,* the Spirit of God, really encompasses everything while *neshamah,* the spirit of man, is an expression or an extension of *Ruwach;* thus confirming the Word of God in Genesis 1:26: ". . . Let us make man in our image . . . ." The word for God in this Scripture is *Elohim,* which is plural. The doctrine of the Trinity is heavily implied by its usage.

Neshamah, the Hebrew-Chaldean word for the spirit of man, only appears twice in the Old Testament—in Job 26:4 and Proverbs 20:27. In Job 26:4 we read, "To whom hast thou uttered words? and whose spirit came from thee?" In the preceding verse of this chapter, we read the comments of Bildad, the Shuhite. He is declaring the power and sovereignty of God. He directs his conversation to Job, and begins to rebuke him, calling him a worm. Bildad was looking at the circumstances, and was forming his own opinion based on those circumstances. He was pronouncing judgment on Job, and implying that Job had no right to righteousness.

In *The Living Bible* paraphrase, we read,

> How can mere man stand before God and claim to be righteous? Who in all the earth can boast that he is clean? God is so glorious that even the moon and the stars are less than nothing as compared to Him. How much less is man, who is but a worm in His sight? (Job 26:4-6).

Bildad was making these comments to Job because he was convinced that Job had committed some terrible sin and was trying to evade his guilt. Bildad was reminding Job that he couldn't stand up to God, and in God's eyes, Job was less than a worm. But Bildad was wrong because God had called Job righteous (Job 1:8). Job was saved by faith unto the promise of Jesus (Gen. 3:15).

Job answered Bildad in chapter 26, verses one through three. In effect, he says, "Thanks for helping me with your encouraging and comforting word when I was down and out." Job was mocking Bildad for his ignorance. He goes on to state in verse three, "you have already made up your mind that I don't know anything, and you have already declared my guilt."

Job 26:4, according to the Amplified Bible, states, "With whose assistance have you uttered these words? And whose spirit inspired what came forth from you?" Job was, in effect, saying to Bildad, "How can you judge me? You call me unrighteous because you are speaking from a degenerate spirit. You certainly did not speak from *neshamah,* (the born-again spirit of man) or else you would not have spoken of me in that way."

Neshamah is the born-again state of man. Man that is able to stand in the presence of God, because he is made in His image and likeness. Job had an inner sense that told him Bildad was not speaking truth. Job was operating in his regenerated spirit by faith. In fact, he was so sure about it that he responded directly from his spirit. The word that is used for spirit here is the word *neshamah,* which is translated as regenerated or born-again man.

Proverbs 20:27 records the only other time when *neshamah* (spirit of man) is used in the Old Testament: "The spirit of man is the lamp of the Lord, searching all the innermost parts of his being" (NAS). The word "being" can be used synonymously with soul.

Genesis 2:7 records that God breathed into the nostrils of man, and he became a living soul. "The innermost parts of his being" indicates that the Scripture is referring to man's soul. The word spirit (*neshamah*) is referring to the born-again spirit of man. This spirit is created in the image and likeness of God, and is the lamp of God. Only regenerated man can be legally associated with God. Unregenerated man cannot be in the presence of God. The new-creation spirit, with the help of the Holy Spirit residing in him, will be able to search the soul, and correct whatever needs to be corrected by the Word of God. The written Word becomes the vehicle to produce the *rhema* (spoken word), and causes our soul to be renewed. With the renewing of our soul, understanding comes. Understanding brings desire, and desire engages the will to act. Manifested action is the result of the relationship of spirit, Word and the power of man's will working together. The Spirit of God operating in man's spirit, and the Word of God operating in man's soul, will effect the power of man's will to bring all things to fruition.

In the New Testament, the Greek word that is used for spirit is *pneuma.* It is defined as a current of air, blast of air, breath or a breeze. It can be described as vital, principle, mental disposition, super, an angel, God, Christ the Spirit, Holy Spirit, or Spirit mind. An example of the characteristics of this word is found in Acts 2:2: "And suddenly there came a sound from heaven as of a rushing mighty wind, and it filled all the house where they were sitting." The Greek word for wind in this passage is *pneuma,* which is translated as spirit. The Holy Spirit is described as being a mighty wind. The actual Greek word for wind is *anemos,* which literally means to toss from the four quarters of the earth; east, west, north, and south. What the disciples were experiencing was not the actual wind, but something similar to the effect the physical wind would have. The Word of God is complete and perfect, and every word is put exactly where the Holy Spirit wanted it to be. Reading the Bible for the purpose of guidance in your life is common, but when you *study* the Bible, you put yourself into another dimension. Carefully studying the Scriptures requires you to go into a deeper understanding of words and their application to the particular event or events that are recorded in the Word.

In the Acts chapter 27, there is a classic example of

what I am saying. The entire chapter of Acts 27 involves a windstorm. Every time the word "wind" is used, it is translated from the Greek word *anemos,* which refers to the wind as we know it, as it pertains to the environment. But in verse 40, a change in usage takes place. The word "wind" here is translated from the word *pneuma.*

Let's take a closer look at this portion of Scripture. The first part of Acts 27:40 states, "And when they had taken up anchors, they committed themselves unto the sea . . . ." What Luke was saying, in effect, at this point was, "We did all that we knew to do in the natural." The verse goes on to say that they "loosed the rudder bands, and hoisted up the mainsail to the wind." As we stated before, the Greek word *pneuma,* used here means Spirit. Luke is saying that now that we have done all that we could do, we are letting go and hooking up with God. He hooked up the mainsail to the Holy Spirit. The verse concludes with the words "and made toward shore." Notice that the action is in the past tense. Luke was speaking as though he had already achieved the shore. He was speaking the faith of the vision that he had received as if it was already done.

An interesting turn of events occurs in Acts 27:41. The ship hit a sandbar and ran aground. The bow of the ship stuck fast, while the stern was exposed to the violence of the waves and began to break apart. Every time you hook up with God, the enemy is going to raise his ugly head. There will always be a battle, but when you are hooked up with God, you are already a winner because the battle has already been won.

God had spoken to Paul and told him that no one would perish, but at that moment, it appeared as though they were doomed. The ship's mainsail, however, was hooked up to the wind (the Holy Spirit), and He was in control. The Spirit of God called out directions through the centurion, and we see the complete victory taking place in verse 44 ". . . and so it was that they all escaped safely to land" (NKJV).

Summary: Man was created in the image, and after the likeness of God. Man is a spirit-being (Gen. 1:26). God put man's spirit being into a body (Gen. 2:7). Man was a spirit-being like God, but operating from a physical body. We see man acting like God, His Father, in Genesis chapter 2, verses 19 and 20. God created all the animals and brought them to Adam to be named, and Adam named them all. This was an awesome accomplishment. Man was acting like God, His Father.

In Genesis 3:6, we see man's fall from his spiritual state. Because of his disobedience to God's Word, he became separated from God. His spirit was dead unto God, and his soul, which is part of the spirit, would now be influenced by what he would feel through his body, because this is the part of him that sinned.

In Genesis 3:15, God's grace and mercy come forth. God speaks His Word that He would send a Redeemer into the universe, and this promise becomes active by faith. Man was restored by and to the promise of Jesus. Adam and Eve would have the opportunity to be saved through the promise of the Redeemer, and we see the evidence of this in Genesis 3:21 where it is recorded that God clothed Adam and Eve with skins. God sacrificed the animals as a type or shadow, or a preview of the coming sacrifice of Jesus. The blood was the atonement for the sinful disobedient nature of man, and the skins were a type and shadow of the redemption of man's body. To paraphrase First Peter 2:24, "By Jesus' stripes we are healed and made whole."

Luke 2:7 shows the beginning manifestation of Genesis 3:15: Jesus is born. John 19:30 is the completed manifestation of Genesis 3:15: Jesus hangs on the cross. He is pierced through His side with a sword, and His blood flows from His side and enters into the ground. He then utters these last words, "It is finished." What God spoke in Genesis 3:15 is finished in John 19:30. God spoke forth the Word, and His Word is Spirit and truth.

The Word was Spirit (not seen) when God spoke in Genesis 3:15, and became truth (seen) when manifested in John 19:30. Hebrews 1:3 states, "Who being the brightness of his glory, and the express image of his person, and upholding all things by the word of his power . . . ." Notice that the Bible states that He upholds all things by His Word. His Word is Spirit and is eternal. His Word is always present as He always is. Every time His Word manifests, it is truth. Christ was the Word from the very beginning. He was always present. Jesus became the Word manifested (John 1:14), and He is truth. Truth is something you can see.

3

Two Kinds of Wisdom

God is good, and everything He created is good. The devil is the master deceiver, and he perverts everything God created. God speaks the truth, for He is truth. The devil speaks lies, for he is a liar.

Unfortunately, there are many things that are happening in the lives of Christians that are true but not good. Truth isn't always positive. If a person is afflicted with an illness, the illness itself cannot be denied, but its right to exist must be denied.

The truth will be established by what your action is focused upon. If you are positive, the truth will be positive. If you are negative, the truth will be negative. The Word of God is irrefutable it demands that we operate by faith. Hebrews 11:6 tells us that without faith it is impossible to please Him. Everything He does for us is done on the basis of our faith. Faith is the confident assurance and the title deed to the things hoped for. It is the certainty that what we hope for is waiting for us, even though we cannot see it. Faith is complete trust in God. It involves taking God at His Word and asking no questions. Faith goes beyond reason. It believes without needing to understand why. Faith is a gift of God that comes by hearing, and hearing by the Word of God (Rom. 10:17). Faith is positive, and whatever is not of faith is sin (Rom. 14:23). Sin is negative and will always cause failure.

God declared that man is in dominion over all of the earth (Gen. 1:26). Man is the *only* power on this earth, and he has the right to change or alter anything that is happening to him. Man is responsible for his actions, and whatever happens in his life is the result of the decisions he makes, voluntarily or involuntarily.

Hosea 4:6 states, "My people are destroyed for lack of knowledge . . . ." Knowledge brings understanding. Understanding is the ability to comprehend, to apply a concept, and to teach someone else how to carry it out. Knowledge is the accumulated facts about anything. There are two kinds of knowledge—God's knowledge, which is the Word of God; and the world's knowledge, which is the knowledge possessed by natural man. Natural man is unregenerated man, the man who is not born-again. He operates solely from his senses.

Not all worldly knowledge, however, is from the devil. Some worldly knowledge is beneficial and can be profitable. Even Jesus told us to learn from the children of the world by learning how they acquire knowledge to become successful. Remember, God created man and his mind, and when man uses his being to do good, good will come forth. There are many people who are not born-again who do good and come up with many good devices to produce good, but they could do even better if they would realize that God is the source of all good and give Him the credit for their accomplishments.

Satan's knowledge is always evil—his desire is to do evil. Evil will destroy you. It sometimes has an appearance of good, but its main purpose is destruction. Satan is the head of the kingdom of evil, and he is good at what he does. Jesus told us that the kingdom of Satan is united. Its citizens are working together for evil, and their main goal is to destroy man and God's goal for man. The devil's nature is to steal, kill and destroy.

Man knows how to devise methods to mine silver and refine gold, to dig iron from the earth, and to process the earth's minerals in many ways which will benefit humanity. Man knows how to insert light into darkness, so that a mine shaft can be sunk deeply into the earth to explore the earth and bring forth the treasures stored there. He knows how to find sapphires and gold dust and treasures that no one has ever seen before. He knows how to tear apart flinty rocks and how to overturn the roots of mountains. He drills tunnels in the rocks to lay bare precious stones. Man dams up streams of water and pans gold from them. These kinds of knowledge are all good. They benefit man and are needed to live in this world, but they are examples of man's natural knowledge.

The Bible instructs us to seek the Kingdom of God and His righteousness first, and all of the other things will be added unto us (Matt. 6:33). The only true knowledge is the knowledge of God; which, when applied, becomes the wisdom of God. The only true wisdom is the Word of God applied to the everyday practical lives of people. The success of the Word in one's life is measured by the results received from the application of the knowledge of the Word to the person's physical abilities and attributes.

Let's look closely at Matthew 6:33. The first part of the verse states, "Seek ye first the kingdom of God." What is the Kingdom of God? Where is the Kingdom of God? A kingdom is a place with an environment and atmosphere that always take on the character of the person or persons involved. The Scripture emphatically states that we are to seek the Kingdom of God. So, let us take inventory of our knowledge of God to determine and recognize God's Kingdom.

In Mark 10:17-18, there is the account of the rich young man who came to Jesus to ask about eternal life. He said to Jesus, "Good Master, what shall I do that I may inherit eternal life?" Jesus answered his question with a question: "Why callest thou me good? there is none good but one, that is, God."

Here Jesus gives us our first key to the Kingdom. The Greek word that is used for good is *agathos,* which is used here as a noun. This was very unusual because nouns don't describe nouns. Adjectives describe nouns. The word that is used to describe *agathos* is *kalos*, which means beautiful, valuable, virtuous, honest, satisfying, well, worthy, and perfect. An adjective will describe a noun as to what it can do, but a noun is the source of what it does. God doesn't only *do* good, but He *is* good. His nature is good, well, worthy, perfect. Everything He does comes from this nature. He can't be anything but good. Jesus is giving us a glimpse of the Father through this Scripture.

Philippians 4:8 tells us,

> Finally brethren, whatsoever things are true, whatsoever things are honest, whatsoever things are

> just, whatsoever things are pure, whatsoever things are lovely, whatsoever things are of good report; if there be any virtue, and if there be any praise, think on these things.

Colossians 3:1-3 states,

> If ye be risen with Christ, seek those things which are above, where Christ sitteth on the right hand of God. Set your affection on things above, not on things on the earth. For ye are dead, and your life is hid with Christ in God.

In James 3:17-18 it is written,

> But the wisdom that is from above is first pure, then peaceable, gentle, and easy to be entreated, full of mercy, and good fruits without partiality, and without hypocrisy. And the fruit of righteousness is sown in peace of them that make peace.

In James 1:17 it says, "Every good and perfect gift is from above, and cometh down from the Father of Lights, with whom is no variableness, neither shadow of turning."

In 2 Timothy 3:16 we read, "All scripture is given by inspiration of God and is profitable for doctrine and reproof, for correction, for instruction in righteousness."

Proverbs 3:5-6 states, "Trust in the Lord with all thine heart; and lean not unto thine own understanding. In all thy ways acknowledge him, and he shall direct thy paths."

Although we don't always understand how the Word

works, and can't fully understand how God inspires us or how He inspired the writers of the Scriptures to write them, if the Word says that something is so, it is settled whether we believe it or not. Therefore, because of Mark 10:17, Philippians 4:8, Colossians 3:1-3, James 3:17-18, James 1:17, 2 Timothy 3:16 and Proverbs 3:5-6, we can come to the beginning of an understanding of God. He is a good God, and everything He does and gives is good. He is not capable of evil because it would violate His nature. He is perfect, without a flaw or blemish. All He knows is goodness, and all that He wants for us is good.

In the Old Testament, God instructed the children of Israel not to come near the holy mountain lest they become consumed and die (Exod. 19:21). In man's natural state, he cannot be in the presence of God, no matter how good his natural state may appear.

The enemy, the devil, is a master deceiver. The Bible reveals that the devil comes like an angel of light and has an appearance of good, but he is evil. In these present times, many are being deceived because of New Age religions that teach that man is good in himself and he doesn't need God. He can do whatever he wants just as long as he feels he is not doing anything wrong. The Bible speaks of this as man doing what is right in his own eyes. This concept teaches that man is his own righteousness, according to the works that he accomplishes. This is a totally erroneous concept, and it is doomed for failure. Jesus spoke of this concept to His disciples in Luke 17:26-30, when He recounted the events that occurred in the days of Noah and Lot. He said that the people ate, drank, married, and did exactly what they wanted to do without any concern about God. So they doomed themselves to the destruction that is described in the Bible. History has a way of repeating itself, and today we see the same attitudes that prevailed in the days of Noah and Lot.

Anything that is not backed up with the Word of God will fail, even though for a while it may have an appearance of being successful.

The wisdom of God is acquired through the knowledge of His Word. It is not found among the elements of the earth nor can it be purchased by the riches of the world. All the wealth of the world cannot buy the wisdom of God. Wisdom is a gift of God, and it was purchased for us by the blood of Jesus, the Lamb. Our acceptance and reception of His sacrifice brings us into the position of acquiring this wisdom. It is free. The only thing we have to do is to receive it.

The Word of God is His Covenant to us. All the promises in His Word are ours, but there is a condition attached to receiving them: we must acknowledge Jesus Christ as our Lord and Savior (Rom. 10:9-10) and commit our ways unto Him.

How do we commit our ways unto Jesus Christ? How do we learn His ways? Where is His Kingdom expressed? In the WORD. Living according to the uncompromised Word of God is what it means to live in the kingdom.

We have to keep God and His character in mind. God says, "Thy kingdom come . . . on earth as it is in heaven" (Luke 11:2, author's paraphrase). In heaven there are only good things. There is no sickness, poverty, or lack. So on this earth, according to God's Word, we should be living in complete health, wealth, and ongoing prosperity.

The inspired Word of God says that we are kings and priests unto God. Are you living like a king? If not, it is not God's fault. He has given us all that we could ever need, but *we* must *seek* and *receive.* If there is no manifestation, we are to seek wisdom, accept the answer by faith (James 1:5), and apply Hebrews 11:1, "Now faith is the substance of things hoped for, the evidence of things not seen." This brings the unseen into the realm of the seen.

4

The Heart of Man

Man is a spirit-being. He has a soul, and his spirit and soul operate from his physical body. Man is not a triune being. He is only one being: spirit-man. The total nature of man operates in this complexity of spirit, soul and body. The soul of man is also comprised of three areas: his conscious mind, his preconscious mind, and his subconscious mind. The heart of man is found in his soul area. The word "heart" is literally translated from *lieb* or *nephesh* in Hebrew-Chaldean. The Greek counterpart is *psuche.* From this root word we get our English word *psyche,* which means soul. Both the original Hebrew and Greek describe the word "heart" as being the seat or center of man's intellect, emotions and will.

The *conscious mind* is the part of the soul that is aware of what is happening at the present time. It has only the ability to comprehend and receive information. It does not maintain memory.

The *preconscious mind* is aware of all the surrounding

conditions when the conscious mind is operating. The preconscious mind is the part of you where your memory is located. It memorizes everything from the environment around you, such as sounds, sights, and smells. The preconscious mind memorizes names, dates, Scriptures, etc. The preconscious mind has memory banks, and can be used extensively if trained and disciplined properly. It can store and recall details at any given time, much like a computer.

The *subconscious mind* is the very basis of man's life. The Bible calls the subconscious mind "the heart of man." The heart of man is the center of man's intelligence, emotions and will.

Here is an illustration of how the heart works. The conscious mind receives all the information through the body senses, which are seeing, hearing, smelling, tasting, and touching. The details, such as size, distinctiveness, depth and awareness development, are passed to the preconscious mind where it is stored in the memory banks. The intelligence, which is all the data that has been processed in the preconscious mind, is then passed into the subconscious mind—or what the Bible calls the "heart of man."

The *constant* processed accumulation of this causes the subconscious mind to produce a picture-like experience. This is imagination. This experience will develop according to the familiarity of the data. If it is repeated over and over again, the heart will believe it and develop confidence (faith) in it.

Faith is an experience, and the seed of this experience begins in the heart. The more distinct the picture, the more powerful the experience. The experience now becomes real inside of you, and will cause the emotional part of your heart to operate. The emotional part of your heart will produce a feeling which will result in the will—the power source—producing or manifesting the experience in the physical realm.

The Bible says in Joshua 1:8,

> This book of the law [the Word] shall not depart out of thy mouth; but thou shalt meditate therein day and night, that thou mayest observe to do according to all that is written therein: for then thou shalt make thy way prosperous, and then thou shalt have good success.

The key word in this Scripture is "meditate." Many people confuse the word meditate with memorization. Memorization only enters into the preconscious mind, where it is stored as information. This information is knowledge only. Knowledge in itself is not capable of acting out or having a feeling. Many Christians operate from their preconscious mind. They think they are doing the Word, but they are only reviewing the facts they already have stored in their memory, which is their preconscious mind. This is called "mental assent."

Meditating is digesting what you have already heard by repeating it over and over again within yourself continuously. By doing this, the words congeal and are processed into picture-like experiences in the subconscious mind (in the heart) where confidence is built up (faith), and this process causes an emotional desire. This desire engages the will to act upon it, which will produce an experience or feeling. This has now become a part of you. You have made it part of your life, and it will be with you forever.

The Hebrew-Chaldean word for meditation is *hagah,* and it means to mutter, roar, murmur, ponder, speak, study, talk, imagine, and muse. Webster's Dictionary defines "meditate" as: "To contemplate or examine attentively or deliberately, think carefully about, consider carefully, watchful attention, supervision, closely attentive to details."

If we closely examine all of these descriptions, we will find that meditation is much more involved than what the average person thinks. The Hebrew-Chaldean's definition begins with "to mutter." Muttering something means to repeat it over and over again in a low voice, or in your mind. Sometimes, it may help some people to roar out their meditation. The loudness keeps their attention focused on what they want to remember. Murmuring, in this usage, would have the same effect as muttering.

Pondering is the next step in this process. When you ponder something, you examine it attentively by going over and over it. You roll it over in your mind, observing all the points involved. You will then begin to study it, and become more involved in the details. Studying will affect the desire to communicate. The more communicative that you allow the meditation to become, the more effective it will be. It will be so real that the meditation will begin to take on picture form. Words will be transformed into picture-like images in your imagination. Picturing requires the use of your imagination. (Note the relationship between the words "image" and "imagination.")

For the purpose of clarification, let's assume that our imagination is like a large television screen. Your television set is the receiver of the signals that are transmitted from the television station to your house. The signals are received by the television set, and are projected into picture form on the screen. These signals are received in tiny little increments. If you were to observe them in slow motion, you would see them appear as tiny little dots forming together from the top and going across in linear manner in subsequent order until the whole screen was filled to the form of the picture being received. This process is going on at such an accelerated speed that it is impossible for the natural eye to see it happening. This example can also be applied to the functioning of the soul as the Word is received in the heart. The digested or meditated Word is transmitted to the television screen of the imagination. As the Word is being processed through meditation by the procedure that has been mentioned previously, it is then sent on to the "imagination" (screen) part of the heart. It is received in the imagination in the same manner as signals are received in our television sets at home. The digested Word is received in the imagination in tiny increments from the top and goes across in linear form and subsequent order until the picture is complete.

The time it takes to complete the picture depends upon the amount of completed meditation you have processed. This, in turn, is determined by the amount of knowledge that you have acquired to meditate on. The Word of God is a personal matter for each of us. We are responsible for inputting the Word in our lives.

Our desire for success can only be realized by our active participation. No one can make the Word work for us. God has given us His ministry gifts—apostles, prophets, evangelists, pastors and teachers—for the perfecting of the saints, for the work of the ministry, for the edifying of the Body of Christ. (See Ephesians 4:11-12.) Notice that these gifts are for *the perfecting of the saints.* Every born-again believer is a "saint." Each one is responsible for his own perfection (completion), but we have those who were sent by God to bring forth His Word to us. When you receive the Word and process it through meditation, it will become part of you by entering into the imagination of your heart. When this happens, the Word becomes alive because it is now part of you. You see yourself as God sees you through the molding of the Word. With this confidence, we then engage the will, which is the power source within us, to bring forth and manifest the conquering Word in our lives. We can apply this process to every area of our lives.

Here's a practical example of how this works. Almost every driver has experienced some apprehension when he first learned to drive. The first step in learning how to drive is to acquire knowledge about driving. This knowledge is received and accepted in the conscious mind, and processed through the preconscious mind, where it is deposited into the memory banks. The knowledge received into the preconscious mind now becomes the basis for meditation. Meditation requires that the knowledge be digested thoroughly by observing every detail over and over again, or until it becomes a reality. At this point, the processed knowledge is transmitted to the imagination of the heart, where it is converted into picture form and now becomes the beginning of an experience. This experience must now be put into an action. The action begins when the information or processed knowledge is applied through the physical senses by an act of the will. This becomes understanding. Understanding is putting knowledge into action. Now driving the car has become part of the person. It has become an experience that is programmed into the heart forever, or until the person changes it. The more the person practices driving, the more efficient they become. Driving a car will eventually become instinctive and automatic.

The Bible says in Romans 10:17, "So then faith cometh by hearing, and hearing by the word of God." When you hear or read the Word of God, it is received into your conscious mind, where it is then filtered through to your preconscious mind. Your preconscious mind stores it in your memory banks, and then it is processed and released to the subconscious mind— or heart—where it is formed into pictures. The process is much like that of a slide projector. The information received from the preconscious mind comes in picture form into the heart, and is ready to be projected into action by stimulating the emotions to engage the will to act.

The Bible tells us that the issues of life emanate from the heart (Prov. 4:23). Your heart—or subconscious— will produce life or death to your being. Life is achieved when you receive positive true knowledge and turn it into action to become part of you. This is called "following through." Joshua 1:8 says, "Meditate on the Word day and night, observe and do, then thou shall make thy way prosperous, and thou shalt have good success" (author's paraphrase).

Chapter one, verse seven of Joshua records that the Lord told him, "Only be thou strong and very courageous, that thou mayest observe to do according to all the law, which Moses my servant commanded thee . . . ." Notice the words, "observe to do." This means to bring knowledge into your mind. Observing requires you to be conscious of something and to concentrate. Concentration engages the conscious mind, and this is the beginning of the development of a life experience. Joshua was also told to be strong and very courageous. This indicates that you have to be attentive to receive the Word, and courageous enough to apply it to your heart.

Proverbs 4:20-22 states,

> My son, attend to my words; incline thine ear to my sayings. Let them not depart from thine eyes; keep them in the midst of thine heart. For they are life unto those that find them, and health to all their flesh.

There are two very important principles in these verses. The first one is "keep them in the midst of thine heart." The Lord is referring to His Word being kept in the center of the heart. The center of the heart is the emotional part of the heart (the seat of desire), which produces feelings. This is where the "will of man" is situated. Production of any action requires the will to be engaged. The will responds only to a definite confidence that is built up by processed, acquired, accumulated knowledge. God is telling us that we are to have the Word processed and ready to be used whenever the occasion arises.

The other important principle is that when we apply the developed Word from the center of our hearts, it will produce life, and it will also produce health to all of our flesh. This is a definite indication of the fact that the Word has to be developed within us. It has to be part of us. We must become a living-Word person. Speaking the Word doesn't necessarily make you a living-Word person. It's a beginning, but to become a living-Word reality requires that you do Proverbs 3:5-6 completely: *"Trust* in the Lord with all thine heart, and lean not unto thine own understanding. In all they ways acknowledge him, and he shall direct thy paths" (italics mine). Study God's Word and take it as He says (not what you think He says). Then put it to work in the process that was just explained. It's guaranteed to work—guaranteed by God, and He never fails.

Joshua 1:8 also tells us to meditate on the Word *day and night.* Meditating is not memorizing. To meditate is to picture (or see) it. Memorization is done in the preconscious mind, while meditation is done in the subconscious mind—in the heart. Memorization is repetitious, and meditation is creative. You can only create in your heart because this is where the issues of life come from. Memorization can help you to meditate, by bringing forth information that actualizes the development of the Word into a living picture of reality in the imagination part of your heart. The combination of your conscious mind, preconscious mind, and subconscious mind (heart), all involved in processing the Word, results in a desire that responds with an emotion. This in turn engages the will to act, to produce a life experience through your physical being which then will become part of you forever. Perfection, maturity, and success only come when you do this over and over again. "So then faith cometh by hearing, and hearing by the Word of God" (Romans 10:17).

Here's what we learned from Joshua 1:8 in a five-step process.

Observe to do: Conscious mind. (Acquiring knowledge.)

Meditate: Preconscious to subconscious mind.

Observe to do according: Subconscious mind (heart). Acquired knowledge processed in picture-like action.

Thou shalt make thy way: Action produced because of desire.

Thou shalt have success: Engaging of the will to enact power.

This completes the "follow through" part of the process of issuing life to your being. Notice and observe that all the steps have to be completed in order for you to have success. Remember, you could bring a great deal of knowledge into the conscious mind and have an abundance of the awareness of the Word, and still nothing would happen. Why? Because this is only "head knowledge." You must meditate on the Word, bringing it into your subconscious (heart), where the actual birth begins. The heart is where creative life starts. Only after full maturity is developed will success be achieved.

Head knowledge applies to all experiential aspects of life. Memorization, or head knowledge, is extremely important, and without it, heart knowledge cannot be achieved. Heart knowledge is the understanding of head knowledge, and the ability to process it through the senses. An example of head-knowledge life application can be explained as follows. Many professors, or vocational teachers, are excellent in teaching the facts or knowledge pertaining to their vocation or profession, but if they were to actually work in it, they might be helpless. They have an abundance of head knowledge, but no heart knowledge. Such teachers have not followed completely through. They have head knowledge only. The heart knowledge requires them to put into action what they know, and this knowledge must be completed through the sensory or physical part of them. They are either unable to see themselves doing so or may not have the desire to do it. Yet, these same professors or vocational teachers can produce excellent success in others.

In watching the Olympics in 1992, I observed the athletes performing their feats. Every part of their bodies were operating with the intensity and purpose of their desire to perform with excellence. Some athletes spend hours meditating (in their hearts) and birthing new ways to perfect their performances. They literally *see* themselves performing with excellence over and over again in their hearts; by this means, they are observing what could be improved, and they are doing it. To meditate, you must observe—that is, see yourself doing or having whatever it is you desire.

Observing requires calling upon the preconscious part of the soul. As you recall, this is the area where the memory of facts—with their distinctiveness, depth, and developed awareness—is stored. When one wants to improve himself, he has to observe what he could do to improve. The first course of action to be taken is to recall from the memory banks (preconscious mind) all the knowledge that is stored there regarding this experience. He takes this information and compares it to the action that he is doing. He may at this time become aware of a better way of doing it because of the confidence that he has developed in himself. He then makes the necessary corrections in his preconscious mind. The correction is then stored and processed into the subconscious mind (heart), where it will develop into the corrected action, and will manifest itself through the physical body.

The heart acts out an action. The heart does not get involved with thinking or concentration, it just responds. An example of this is the account of the person learning how to drive a car. Once you have the experience in your heart, you will act upon that experience all the time without concentration or thinking. The heart automatically involves the preconscious mind by tapping into it for the necessary information that it may need to complete the action, thus producing success that will make its way prosperous.

For example, the Apostle Paul talks about athletes running a race. He makes references to the weights they wore around their ankles. These weights were worn while they were training to produce strength and muscular dexterity. They made the runner very tired, and more than likely, the extra weight often made him want to quit. What would keep the runner going, however, was the success that he saw in his heart. He saw himself as a winner. As the picture grew stronger, he became more confident. He observed—with the eye of his heart—his every movement, and pushed on to perfect his performance. When the day of the race came, he would take off the weights and begin to run. The legs that had been trained with the weights suddenly had the freedom of no weights. They flew with extraordinary speed that was produced by a picture of victory that was developed in his heart.

The preconscious mind was corrected to include the awareness of the weights when the training was started. It then informed the subconscious (heart) of this "developed awareness," and the heart incorporated this information into the involved muscle fiber of the man's body. Every muscle, tissue and blood vessel that was needed for running knew that the weights were on, and they were ready to run with the weights on. Suddenly, they were gone, but the heart acts as it has been taught, with the weights on. The man runs twice as fast because his subconscious mind is acting on the only knowledge it has, causing the body to run twice as fast subconsciously because of the absence of the weights. The body had no choice but to go faster. The heart could only act on what had been programmed into it, and that was to run as if there were weights on. The body is flexible. It will do whatever the heart wants it to do or not to do. This feat would seem like an "impossibility," but what was conceived in the heart, by putting pressure on the body, produced the miracle or impossible feat. This is how we must act on God's Word in our lives as well. By so doing, we will run life's race with the confidence that leads us to victory.

In James 1:2, we read, "My brethren, count it all joy when ye fall into divers temptations." Trials and temptations are the circumstances of life. They are a real part of life. By developing the Word in our hearts, we will be able to overcome these trials. It is the developed Word that will manifest conquering action over the circumstances, and this is what will count for joy.

In John 10:10, we are told that Satan is the thief. He comes to steal, kill and destroy. This is his nature. When we begin to meditate on the Word, and the Word is developed in our hearts, Satan will come to test us. Remember, trials and tests are for the Word's sake. Satan begins to bring pressures to bear through various circumstances and situations to test the Word that is being developed in our hearts. For example, he may cause sickness or a financial crisis to erupt. One's first reaction is to give in to the circumstances, which is the natural thing to do. After all, we have been taught all of our lives that seeing is believing. But the Word of God teaches that we must believe first, then we will see. Just like the runner in training, we must see ourselves as winners who are overcoming the circumstances. We must press on.

The beginning of any manifested action takes place in the subconscious (heart) of man. All manifested experiences, whether good or bad, are recorded in the heart. The more that we manifest an experience (good or bad), the more confident or discouraged we will become. The successes will produce confidence, and the failures will produce discouragement. This is why the Bible says to count it all joy when we fall into various trials. It gives us opportunities to invoke the Word to produce positive manifested actions for our subconscious (heart) to act upon at later dates.

In John 10:10, Jesus tells us about Satan. He refers to him as the thief. "The thief comes to steal, kill, and destroy" (author's paraphrase). Satan comes to steal the Word, or your confidence in the Word. If he can *steal* your confidence, he is able to *kill* your joy. If he succeeds in killing your joy, he can destroy your strength, because the Word advises us that the "joy of the Lord is your strength" (Neh. 8:10). When Satan destroys your strength, you don't feel like going on. He then comes in for the kill. He brings on discouragement to break down your will. Your will is your power source. If he can affect your will, he can stop your action, and instead of acting on the Word, you will react to the circumstance.

See how the same five-step process that produces life can also produce death when it is applied negatively.

Observe to do: Doubt received in the conscious and preconscious mind.

Meditate: Transmission from the preconscious to subconscious in picture form.

Observe to do according: Emotional feelings of depression.

Thou shalt make thy way: Action taken in the negative produces death, not life.

Thou shalt have success: Causing the will to react to the circumstances.

Jesus said in the latter part of John 10:10, "But I have come to give you life and life more abundantly" (author's paraphrase). This shows how flexible the heart (subconscious) of man is. It does not know right from wrong. The heart will act upon and bring forth whatever you put into it—God's Word or Satan's lies; abundant life or loss, death, and destruction.

5

Man—An Intelligent Being with a Free Will

In Genesis 1:26, the Bible indicates that God created man in His image and after His likeness, and He gave man complete dominion, power, and authority over all of the earth and everything in it. God created man with a free will. In this respect, he was just like God. Because of his free will, he could say yes or no to God. Now the earth had a new ruler, and this ruler was man. Man's will would be and still is today the only power on this earth. This is an established fact from the Word of God.

Chapter 3 of Genesis tells the account of the man's sin and his separation from God. The man and woman were deceived by the devil, and they delivered *their* authority to the *devil.* The devil neither had nor has authority of his own. It was and still is given to him by man. Luke 4:6 records that the devil said to Jesus, "All this power will I give thee, and the glory of them: for that is delivered unto me; and to whomsoever I will I give it." Notice that it states, "for that is delivered unto me." Satan is giving the real account of what happened in the garden of Eden. He reveals the truth that Adam gave up his right to rule the world system. Satan had to tell the truth because Christ was there when it happened. Satan did not take the authority away from Adam by using power or force. He did it by deception, and he is still working by deception today. He is the master deceiver.

But things are different now. Jesus told his disciples after He had risen from the dead and just before He took His place in heaven,

> All power (*authority* in NKJV) in heaven and on earth was given unto me. I now give it to you. Go, therefore, now and do the things that I did. Lay hands on the sick, cast out demons, speak in other tongues, take up serpents; and if thou drink any deadly thing, it shall not harm you (author's paraphrase of Matthew 28:18 and Mark 16:15-18).

We, the believers and disciples of the Lord Jesus Christ, have been reinstated to the position that God first created man to hold. We were made in His image and likeness with the ability to do what He does and says.

Romans 8:19 tells us that the earth and the whole of creation eagerly awaits ". . . the manifestation of the sons of God." We are His sons. We are the generations of kings. We are kings under Jesus. He is called the King of kings. Another thing that is important about these two portions of Scripture is that Jesus was a man when He walked this earth. He was a human being like you and me, and He was filled and led by the Holy Spirit. He laid down His divinity so He could become our substitute sacrifice. He became like us so that we could become like Him. He took our penalty into hell and paid the price for us. He was born-again by the Spirit of God right from the bowels of hell, and He made an open show of Satan. Jesus stripped him of his authority, reduced him to the state he was in before the Fall, and freed mankind from the curse of sin.

After Jesus finished His work in hell, He rose up, and so completed the final fulfillment of the prophecy that is recorded in Genesis 3:15: "And I will put enmity between thee and the woman, and between thy seed and her seed; it shall bruise thy head, and thou shalt bruise his heel."

Jesus spent forty days on earth after His resurrection. During those forty days He spoke to the apostles and encouraged them. No doubt He told them, "I have done it all. I have fought *your* battle, and I took back the power and authority that Adam gave away. Now I am giving it back to you." And then Jesus promised that He would send them the Holy Spirit. The Holy Spirit would be their God-given helper. He was their insurance policy. He would come and take residence inside of them. He would become part of them, and could not be separated from them.

At this point, I want to reemphasize that when God speaks His Word, He has to stand by it. The authority was given to us, and we, as believers, must will to use it. With this authority, all things are possible. We have the power in our will to believe and do what God says, and it will be done to the extent of our commitment to His Word. We also have the power to say "no," and that will lead us to destruction and doom us to eternal damnation.

Man is an intelligent being with a free will. He must acquire knowledge in order to operate. Acquired knowledge is received only through man's senses, and they are seeing, hearing, smelling, tasting, and touching.

Man is equipped from birth to acquire knowledge. It is incorporated into his DNA cell structure. When conception occurs in the womb through the fertilization of the egg by the male sperm, life begins. This life will take on the characteristics of both the mother and the father. They are formed into a single cell structure from which the whole body is formed.

The first part of the fetus made from the cell structure is the brain. The brain is the center of man's operational functions in his physical body. This single cell contains the ability to produce exactly what is needed to form and maintain the body.

As soon as the brain is formed, every part of the body will develop. The development and maintenance stages will be centered completely in the brain. Within this cell structure is the ability to bring forth the already combined characteristics of both parents, causing the development of the fetus to be formed in the likeness of the mother and father. This tiny DNA structure has the details and all the specifics of the couple involved: the whole body with all its organs; all the hairs on the body; the length of the arms, legs, fingers, toes; the height and fat cells, which determine the height and weight.

Life is given to us by God. The account of how animal and human life was created by God is detailed in Genesis. Animals have no souls—they operate on instinct only. They have no mind. They do have a brain, and their instincts and behavior are directly linked to their brains. The breath of life is incorporated in their instincts. The breath of life in man, however, is in his spirit.

Man is a spirit-being, with a soul which is composed of a conscious mind, preconscious mind, and a subconscious mind (heart). Man has a body, and his body is the dwelling place for his spirit and soul. The spirit of man gives life to the body, but the soul of man operates the body through his brain. The brain is the receiver through which the body performs its delegated and acquired tasks and abilities.

The development of man's mind is contingent upon the development of his brain. When a child leaves his mother's womb, he is equipped with a brain, but it is not developed functionally. His method of communication is primarily emotional—through his feelings. If he is hungry, hurting or uncomfortable, he will cry. The mother will know what his needs are because she is in tune with her child's feelings. The soul of the child is operating, but his brain is not developed enough for him to communicate through it. The development of the brain will eventually allow the soul to become more dominant.

When a child is born, he will bring forth some of the physical characteristics of his parents, but as he progresses he acquires a physical appearance of his own. He will still retain what he has inherited, but will also develop many new characteristics. For instance, a baby may look like his father. He may move his hands, look or squint in the same manner that his father does. These characteristics were part of the DNA cell structure of the father's sperm, and now have become part of the baby. But now the child has a chance to produce and develop his own cells. Life is an ongoing process of producing cells.

Man is continuously producing new cells. As the old ones die, the new cells are created with the current and complete make-up of the individual at the time the cell is being formed. This cell incorporates all of the characteristics, habits and functions of the complete person as he is then. Every cell goes through the same process as it is being formed.

As the child matures, he will continually acquire knowledge. This knowledge, good or bad, is incorporated in each cell along with all of the rest of the characteristics that are involved with the makeup of that person. His life will be whatever he incorporates into that cell when it is created.

This creation is the ongoing process of life. Cell creation is like faith. It is always in the "now," or the present time. Our actions are always governed by thoughts which are expressed in words. What we speak over ourselves, or what is spoken over us by others, have a definite effect in our lives—especially when we *receive* the words. Therefore we are to guard our minds, hearts and mouth with all diligence. Proverbs 18:21 states, "Death and life are in the power of the tongue . . . ."

Until the child reaches the age of reason, he has little control over his life. He will operate from his senses. He has no reasoning power because his brain is not developed enough for his mind to operate through. Children are under the protective care or cover of their parents. This is why the Bible says, "Train up a child in the way he should go: and when he is old, he will not depart from it" (Prov. 22:6)

The way a child should go is the way of the Word of God. The Word is life. Parents should speak the Word over their children as often as physically possible. Children will acquire the knowledge to which they are exposed. If you expose them to negativism, they will develop negativism and carry it to adulthood. Negativism results in fear, doubt, insecurity, and failure. The more the child experiences these qualities, the greater the possibility that he will acquire them because they become fundamental perceptions about himself that become increasingly entrenched in his soul. These negative attitudes will produce after themselves and become attributes of all relationships and everything that is done and said until they are changed.

If you expose a child to the positive aspects of life—the Word of God—he will be full of faith in God, with the knowledge that he has God's ability within himself. As his new cell structure develops daily with the Word of God, he will begin to exert confidence, assurance, and success.

We are the product of many generations of ancestors. Without the Word in our lives, we would become the product of the natural world, and that would be based on negativity. But with the Word in our lives, we will be and do what the Word declares we can do. We are more than conquerors. We can do all things through Christ who lives in us. Anything we lay our hands on will prosper. We are the head and not the tail. We are above and not beneath.

A very important point to remember here is that everyone is responsible for his own salvation. We do not inherit salvation through our physical being. What we do inherit is the good physical characteristics that the New Birth causes us to become. While we can receive characteristics that the faith of Godly parents and grandparents, our salvation depend on us individually accepting and calling upon Jesus to become the Savior of our lives (Rom. 10:9-10).

6

Spirit, Soul, and Body

What is the difference between the soul (mind, preconscious, subconscious) and the body? The body is a shell that houses the spirit and soul of man. The spirit and soul are called the inner man. The body cannot function without the inner man, but the inner man can operate without the body. The body is the vehicle through which the spirit and soul (inner man) operate. It is the invisible (unseen soul and spirit) manifesting through the body to the visible (seen). The body is physical matter and will deteriorate unless there is a living soul operating it. The body eventually dies, but we are promised that it will resurrect, and we will be like Jesus with a perfect body that cannot be corrupted again (Phil. 3:21).

The soul can function without the body and it lives forever. The soul begins life when the sperm fertilizes the egg in the womb of the woman. The process that takes place in the womb of the woman in conception could never happen biologically on its own. If one observes the process of the beginning of life in the womb of a woman, judging by the direction and accurate control of what is happening, this cannot be accredited to chance. It has to be the work of an intelligent Spiritual Being. There is definitely an invisible, intelligent direction involved in the creation of the cells. It governs their proper movement according to the size and shape of the new life that is being formed in the woman.

Man is an intelligent being who is capable of performing and creating extraordinary things because he is created in the image and likeness of his Father, God. Man has the ability to acquire information, process it and apply it to action. This is called intelligence, and it is only found in the heart (subconscious) of man. The brain is only a flesh organ that receives its information from the soul of man in order to operate his body. The brain cannot do anything on its own. Without the soul, the brain will die.

The soul will process every cell of the body, thus giving life to each cell. The breath of life comes from the spirit-man and emanates through the soul into the cell structure, causing the body to become alive. This life is an ongoing process that causes the cells to duplicate themselves. This duplication continues life in the body.

The soul receives whatever you put into it. Your body and life are the result of the acquired knowledge that you observed in life. The quality of this acquired knowledge entering into the conscious mind, and processed through the preconscious and subconscious, will determine the quality of life you will have. The Word of God guarantees our success, but acquiring it is up to each one of us individually. We must bring the

Word into our hearts, and when we do so, it will perform to perfection.

Proverbs 2:1, is confirmation of the above:

> My son, if thou wilt receive my words, and hide my commandments with thee; So that thou incline thine ear unto wisdom, and apply thine heart to understanding . . . ."

The Word is received in the conscious mind. To hide the commandments means to memorize them. This is done and stored in the preconscious mind. "Incline thy ear . . . and apply thy heart to understanding" means to activate the Word into the reality of this physical life, and this is done in the heart. The heart creates, and the will works it out.

Proverbs 2:9-11 tells the result you will receive when you do this:

> Then shalt thou understand righteousness, and judgment, and equity; yea, *every* good path. When wisdom entereth into thine heart, and knowledge is pleasant unto thy soul; Discretion shall preserve thee, understanding shall keep thee (italics mine).

When the Word has been applied to the heart, and it completes the cycle, it becomes an "issue of life." The Bible tells us in Proverbs 4:23: "Keep thy heart with all diligence; for out of it are the issues of life." The issues of life are the experiences that you have. They cannot be the "issues of life" unless you experience them.

When God spoke and breathed life into man (Gen. 1:26-2:7), it was the life of God in man's cells. Man's cells were originally created in the image and likeness of God, and he operated with the mind of God. Man's body was the offspring of God's perfection. His body was created to live forever. The Spirit and life of God flowed freely through the body of man. God is positive and He is life. Death and darkness have no part in Him, and God can have no part of them.

Man's cells began to produce death after the Fall, and slowly his body began to die. It took over 900 years to destroy Adam's body. Satan infiltrated man's cells, and the process of deterioration was introduced. Over the years, through inheritance, the majority of mankind has deteriorated to the point of not living past eighty years.

Man began to receive negative thoughts, and he began to process them in his heart. The heart would process the thoughts into a picture-like action causing the will to act in producing a life leading to death. Each subsequent generation, being further and further removed from the original state of man, caused man to literally die a little more every day. The very process that God had created to produce life would now be in reverse, producing death. Man's very DNA cell structure was now subject to the degenerative influence of Satan.

Now Adam's direction would be changed. After he partook of the tree of the knowledge of good and evil, he would have a new knowledge that never was part of him. This was the knowledge of *self.* This self-knowledge is the nature of Satan. It focuses on self, and on self-gratification through the senses. Satan had taken control of Adam, and he would rule him though his senses—the flesh part of him. God's knowledge and wisdom is in His Word, and man's knowledge is in his senses. The knowledge of the world today is sense structured. This is why the world's point of view is directly contrary to God's point of view.

Man was now going to experience a complete takeover of his thinking capabilities, and he was going to see and experience his downfall. In Genesis 4:1, the account of Eve's conception and birth of Cain is recorded. This took place immediately after they had sinned and were put out of the garden. Cain was born with the cell of fallen man. He was a self-centered man who esteemed only himself. He was envious of his brother, Abel, and the very nature of the devil came forth through him. That nature of *stealing, killing and destroying* came into physical manifestation when Cain killed Abel. Cain wanted what Abel had. He wanted to reap where he had not sown. The characteristics of the devil came alive in man. Man performed the act of Satan in the physical realm.

This pattern would be repeated over and over again to such an extent that God would look at man and wish that He had never created him. In Genesis 6:3, it is recorded that God said, "My spirit shall not always strive with man, for that he also is flesh: yet his days shall be an hundred and twenty years."

God was actually saying that man was so much into himself that even He couldn't get to him. But He spoke His Word and said that He would give man 120 years to mend his ways. If God had not spoken that Word at that time, man would have destroyed himself because every man was doing what was right in his own eyes (humanism). Man was operating with the nature of Satan programmed into his cells. He was bent on destroying not only himself, but all of God's creation.

Sodom and Gomorrah are prime examples of man giving in to his flesh. Man became so decadent that he had no regard for life of any kind. He had lost all dignity. Man had engaged in every perversion imaginable. He engaged in all kinds of sexual perversion—from homosexuality to bestiality

In Genesis 18, there is the account of the angels who were sent by God to destroy Sodom and Gomorrah because of the completely corrupted state of those two cities. Lot was sitting at the gate when the angels arrived in the city, and he invited them to come to his home where they could relax for the night.

In Genesis 19:4, we see the corrupt condition of Sodom. It reads, "But before they lay down, the men of the city, even the men of Sodom, compassed the house round, both old and young, all the people from every quarter." Verse five tells their purpose. They wanted to be intimate with the angels because of their great beauty.

The men of Sodom and Gomorrah were unaware that Lot's invited guests were angels. All that they saw were men of great beauty. Man had fallen to his lowest state. Man was created to mate with woman, whereby he would create life. His natural desire was for woman. Now he had become a slave to his physical senses which were governed by Satan, and perversion took over. This decadent life had become a natural way of living. Through this process, man would be causing death to himself instead of life.

Lot began to plead with the men of Sodom, but they would not listen. They were so engrossed in their evil, perverse desires that they tried to force their way into

Lot's house. They were only interested in doing what seemed right in their own eyes. When they tried to force their way in, they were blinded by the angels so Lot and his family could get away. The angels had no choice but to destroy Sodom because there was no good found in it. Evil had taken over man and Sodom, and man was determined to destroy whatever was in his way. He had gone beyond the point of wanting to change.

Satan had deceived man all those years. He was able to program death and destruction into man's life through the process of negative thinking. Man began to operate in a negative cycle instead of a positive cycle. The principle of sowing and reaping was empowered in the negative. When you begin a cycle, it will repeat itself over and over again automatically until you change. Change of direction can only come by a spoken word. If you say or speak something, you will commit yourself to an action. In Genesis 3:15 it is recorded that God said He would send us a Redeemer. Because God spoke His Word in the Garden, man was preserved supernaturally until Jesus came. Jesus is the Christ, the Son of God, who was conceived in Mary by the Holy Spirit. Mary gave flesh to the seed of God, and Jesus, the man, was born.

Now the earth and all of God's creation became a witness to the second perfect man, and that man was Jesus. When Adam was created, he was created in the image and likeness of God. He was perfect and his cell structure was perfect. When he sinned, he was separated from God. He died spiritually. His very nature became as that of the devil, and every person who would be born into the world would be corrupt because they came from the corruptible seed of Adam.

But Jesus was different because He was not born of man, but of God. This time God, through the person of Christ, and through the body of Mary, became Jesus. Jesus, the man, came to take back what Adam, the man, gave away. Although Jesus had all the attributes of God, He could not use them on this earth. He would only act in the authority of a man. Jesus operated on this earth as a manifested Son of God under the guidance and direction of the Holy Spirit.

Jesus' main purpose for being born into the realm of humanity was to free man and bring him back to the state he was in when God created him. Man originally was created full of *power and authority* to reign and rule over all the earth and Satan, but Satan was given this authority by Adam and Eve through deception. There was a sacrifice to be paid, and it had to be a blood sacrifice because it is in the blood that life begins.

We see the first sign of a blood sacrifice in Genesis 3:21. God sacrificed animals. The blood became a temporary covering for the souls of Adam and Eve, and the skins were a covering for their bodies. This blood sacrifice would continue on until the perfect sacrifice of Jesus.

The only sacrifice that would redeem man would be the perfect sacrifice of Jesus. Scientifically, knowing that it is the *sperm* that gives the life that is in the blood, we know that the blood to be shed for the salvation of man, the blood of the sacrificial Lamb, was pure and perfect. This is one reason why Jesus' birth *had* to be of a virgin.

Jesus did not stop at the cross. He went right into hell and paid our penalty. He was quickened and made alive by the Spirit of God. He was born-again from the bowels of hell. The Bible says He made an open show of Satan. He stripped Satan of all his power (Col. 2:15). After He did this, He then rose up to retrieve his Body, and appeared on earth for the very first time as God in Spirit and in the flesh.

Now because Jesus had become the deity of God in a physical being, He had to do the legal and right thing. God is perfect, and He has to stand on His Word. God could no longer function on *earth* because He had given man all authority on this earth (Gen. 1:26). Satan was waiting to see what was going to happen, but Christ was prepared from the beginning of time.

In Mark 16:15-19 and Matthew 28:18-20, Jesus revealed to the whole universe the purpose of His sacrifice and victory over Satan. He restored to man the authority that had been delivered to Satan by Adam. Notice what Jesus said in Matthew 28:18, ". . . All power is given unto me in heaven and in earth." Doesn't that sound strange coming from Jesus? He is God. Power was already His. What did He mean? Jesus was saying that the power and authority that were turned over to Satan were now His, and He was going to restore them back to their rightful owner—man. They were given to man for a purpose, and that purpose was to take authority over Satan and to keep God's creation whole. In effect, Jesus was saying, "Take and restore back to Me what belongs to Me." In that, Jesus was referring to the human race. He goes on to say,

> Go ye therefore, and teach all nations, baptizing them in the name of the Father, and of the Son, and of the Holy Ghost: Teaching them to observe all things

> whatsoever I have commanded you: and, lo, I am with you alway, even unto the end of the world. Amen (Matt. 28:19-20).

Here, Jesus was saying to make disciples of everyone who would receive Him by an act of their free will.

Once Jesus transferred this power and authority to man, He could no longer stay here. He had to resume His rightful place in heaven with the Father. By leaving the earth, He made it possible for the Holy Spirit to come to earth and dwell in man. Jesus is now sitting at the right hand of the Father, waiting for the sons of God (men and women) to manifest so that He (Jesus) can return to earth to rule and reign in His human form. (See Heb. 1:13.)

All authority belongs to man on this earth. In Genesis 1:26, God made man in His image and likeness. He gave man the authority over all of the earth. Man was to rule and reign with power and authority that comes from the nature of love. He knew no evil. All man was aware of was good and perfect. The good and perfect always overcome evil. When your eyes are on the positive, the negative doesn't seem to exist—even though it is all around you.

Whatever man will receive in his heart (subconscious), will manifest in his life. The Word of God, which carries the nature of God, will bring life and abundance to a believer. Your life will be fruitful in all ways. Worldly knowledge—or the knowledge of natural man—will take on the nature of the devil. This thinking is centered on self, and eventually it will cause destruction. We see this happening on a continual basis throughout the Bible. Even today, we see among the believers so much suffering and depression. This is because they are operating in double-mindedness. They believe and then they doubt. This causes a person to become discouraged, and eventually they will want to give in to the circumstance that appears to be overcoming them. (See James 1.)

It is when we are tempted to doubt that we must bring the Word of God into our hearts in a stronger and deeper application than ever before. We must picture ourselves as winners, and actually see ourselves having victory over the circumstances that are surrounding us at that time. Our feelings at that time are not to be followed. The Word is not operated by feelings, but it will produce feelings. According to Hebrews 4:12, God's Word is more powerful than any two-edged sword. It separates soul from spirit. Our soul is the part of us that operates the body. Our soul is the area where the Word of God will produce the emotional feeling that will overcome all natural or worldly emotions: fornication, idolatry, adultery, homosexuality, thievery, covetousness, drunkenness, foul-mouth reviling, slander, and extortion.

Being born-again causes the flesh to die. We no longer have to sin, and since we have this new creation, we can put our flesh down. We do this by receiving the Word in our hearts in order to combat the desires that come from the flesh. The heart produces the desires and emotions for the will to engage the flesh. By having our heart full of the Word, we will be able to create the manifestation to be produced in our flesh. Having done this, the flesh will no longer act in sin, but it will operate in the Word. Thus we become Word-controlled like Jesus was.

Man was created to live forever, and his body was also created to live forever. Originally, because man was created perfect in every way, his cell structure would operate in this perfection. His cells were programmed to produce this perfection which would produce life abundantly. They would never die. The man was created like God; therefore, the Word would be fully operating in him. The Word is full and complete, and there would never have been a need for him to learn anything. We were created in God's image. He is all-knowing. Original man was created just like his God, his Father .

The Fall of the man brought separation and death. This death also manifested in his body. The cells that were originally created to live forever were now introduced to death and destruction. Fortunately, God intervened. He spoke His Word (Genesis 3:15), and gave life to man again. Man's body would still die because his original nature had been reversed. He took on the nature of the devil which was death and destruction. By God speaking the Word, He gave life to every dying cell. As the cells died, new ones erupted to continue to give life to the body.

By this time, man was completely in the power of the devil's deception. He was separated from God, and he was under Satan's total influence. Satan began programming death into every cell that was biologically created by making man speak death over himself. Man, instead of becoming alive, was perpetuating death with each cell that was created. He no longer could see himself like God, but saw himself as the opposite of who he really was. This condition still exists today.

As a born-again child of God, your soul, which is the part of you that controls your body, has to be filled with the knowledge of God. The soul is the operator of the body. The Word of God operating through the soul will produce the experience that will manifest the victory of Jesus on this earth by bringing Christians to their rightful positions, which is to reign as kings under Jesus Christ, the King of kings.

The body itself has no emotions. All emotions are produced by the soul, but all information will come through the senses. The body is the vehicle that God created for man to experience his feelings in the physical realm. Man's body was created to experience only good.

We are told in the Bible that sin dwells in the flesh—that is, in the body. The natural inclination of the body is to desire and experience what is evil. (See Rom. 7:15-17.) The body wants to do evil. It will send signals to the soul that it wants to experience what is sinful. When the soul is renewed to the Word of God, it will refuse to do what the body wants. Instead, the soul will begin to tell the body to do what the Word says, and the body will change its habits. This is not an easy task. The body has been used to having its own way, and it will not give up so easily. There will be a battle, but eventually the Word of God will conquer.

Man's senses originally were a vehicle to expose and show the glory of God on this earth. They were only a minor part of man. Because of the Fall, his senses had now become the major part of him. He would remain in that condition until the coming of Jesus.

The new-creation spirit of man is perfect. The soul, the emotional part of man, has to be renewed because this is the part of man that sinned in the garden. This is the part that pertains to the senses.

Proverbs 4:23 states, "Keep thy heart with all diligence; for out of it are the issues of life." Entrance of the Word into our heart (subconscious) will continually produce life. It will create what is necessary to maintain the body to the perfection that God intended it to have. Proverbs 3:8 states, "It [obedience to the Word] shall be health to thy navel, and marrow to thy bones." Hebrews 4:12 says that "the Word penetrates to the marrow of the bones" (author's paraphrase). Scientists tell us that it is in the marrow of our bones that cells are created. Here in the bone marrow is where life is continuously being created.

As we previously stated, it is out of a renewed heart that the positive issues—or experiences—of life come. So out of a renewed heart, the Word is spoken, and even the marrow in our bones *must* respond. And when bone marrow is functioning in the perfection that God originally intended, the result is health in our cells—the very core of our physical beings. What was dead becomes alive. The degree of the success of this process is determined by the degree of our commitment to the Word. The more we are committed to the Word, the more successful will be this process.

There is authority to be taken, and man has to take it. He must take authority over his body by speaking the Word over it, and commanding the brain to receive it. By taking authority, man is obeying God, and the body will respond. It has to do so because God said it would. We must also exercise patience. James 1:4 states, "But let patience have her perfect work, that ye may be perfect and entire, wanting nothing." We take authority by faith. Then working this faith through patience, and letting patience have its perfect way will produce the manifestation of God's life in us. Maturity of life is having God's Word operating in us naturally.

Hebrews 4:12 in the *Amplified Bible* states that the Word will go to ". . . the deepest parts of our nature, exposing *and* sifting *and* analyzing *and* judging the very thoughts and purposes of the heart." Our thoughts produce our emotions, and eventually what we feel is what we will do. The Word will convict the unbeliever, but it will also challenge the believer. Keep that in mind—*the Word will challenge the believer.* The Word is living and active. It will produce what you allow it to produce. It will change whatever needs to be changed, but it requires an act of your free will to allow the Word to develop in your heart (subconscious) to bring life—abundant life—in you.

The active Word of God, backed by the Sovereign God, can do all things. It will accomplish that which it was sent to do. It was sent to restore us to the position we were created to hold, and that is to be in complete authority and power in heaven and on this earth. The heaven that is mentioned here is not the heaven where God reigns, but the heaven—the outer atmosphere—where Satan has his strongholds. We are to take our authority in that heaven, because Satan no longer has rightful authority. He is ruling by deceit. Romans 8:19-22 tells us that "the whole of creation eagerly moans and groans for the manifestation of the sons of God" (author's paraphrase). Jesus gained the victory for us by His death and resurrection. By accepting His sacrifice and making Him the Lord of our lives, we are born-again. We become a brand-new creation, not a re-creation.

We are created out of something that was not there before. Old things have passed away, and we have become new.

Our purpose now is clear and simple. We are to get back what belongs to God. The earth is calling us to bring it back to the condition that it was in when it was first created. But nothing will happen until the sons of God (born-again men and women) use their authority. Authority must be exercised. It won't work unless you take it and use it.

Our authority is the complete Word of God. On the cross, Jesus said, "It is finished." Now it's up to us to believe what He has done, receive it in our hearts, act upon it, and see it become manifest.

For manifestation to occur in the physical, the Word of God must be brought from our spirit-person through our soul into our body. Understanding of the Word has to be in the soul area first. Understanding is applying the Word to our senses. This will cause us to experience the Word. As the Word is spoken, faith is engaged. Faith is always in the now, the present. Every time you speak the Word, you operate in faith. This is the process that will cause the body to manifest the Word through the senses.

Medical scientists are in the beginning stages of developing a process whereby they can change the cell structure of a person who is suffering from some genetic malfunction. They will remove the malfunctioning gene and replace it with a normal gene. Through this process the cell will be restored to normalcy and begin to produce the proper cell structure. This process has also been experimentally used when a pregnant woman is carrying a baby with a genetic abnormality. Through testing, the baby's exact cell malfunction would be determined, and the doctor removes the defective cell from the unborn baby and replace it with a normal cell. This normal cell begins to reproduce itself, and eventually the baby is restored to complete normalcy and is born normal.

Now if science has proven that the cell structure can be changed through medical intervention, think how much more the Word of God can do. God's Word is His sovereign power. God's Word is alive and active. It is more powerful, exact and complete than any scientist in the world. Fill your heart with the Word. Apply it to your life so that you can be healed and whole right down to the fiber of your physiology. This is the will of God.

Adam and Eve's sin was of the flesh, or what we call senses. The senses are controlled by the soul. The soul is only capable of logic or natural understanding. Anything to do with the senses demands logical reasoning and understanding. While logic and reasoning have their place, the things of the spirit transcend the natural.

Remember, in order for man to respond to the soul, the brain must receive what the soul is sending. At one time, medical scientists stated that man uses only ten percent of his brain, and this was considered genius level. The other ninety percent of the brain is unused. They have no logical answer for this. Even to this date, with all the state-of-the-art equipment, medical science is still puzzled. They have experimented in every way to produce results in this area, but nothing has been accomplished.

The things that human beings have accomplished over the centuries have been astounding. The world's history is resplendent with extraordinary accomplishments and feats. And all this has been done with the use of only ten percent of the brain's capacity—the logical, sense-related part of the brain. What about the other part of the brain, the ninety percent that is unused?

When God created Adam, the glory of God was all around him. Adam's body was only to be the vehicle for his spirit. We inherited the part of Adam that sinned. It became our soul, and is the part of us that is related to our senses (feelings). A human being's soul is operating in the active ten percent part of the brain. I believe that born-again Christians can activate the whole of their brains—that we can tap into the resources of the ninety percent of the brain that is dormant.

Jesus is our example. He was born of flesh and blood. He was born of the Father, and was sinless. He was perfect in every way, and His mind did not have to be renewed. I believe that the whole of Jesus' brain was active—not just ten percent of it. His spirit and soul were in total agreement. The proof of this is in the supernatural things that He did through His body. He walked on the water, multiplied the loaves of bread and fishes, and did many more physical feats that defied all logic. All these things were done through His senses. The spirit-man, if he is in control of the body, would be able to do the same. Jesus told us that we would be doing all these things—and even greater things. (See John 14:12.)

The Word and God are the same, and He never changes. In these last days, God has opened our eyes to a realistic understanding of His Word. Man has finally realized that the kingdom of God is here, and it's about time that we claimed what is ours for the glory of God. But the sound waves will not be heard unless the radio is turned on—and your body will not manifest the glory of God unless your brain (your receiver) is turned on.

Man's authority on earth begins with his authority over himself—spirit, soul and body. Man must speak the Word in order for it to work. Just as God spoke the world into existence by His Word, so we must act like God and speak the Word to bring into existence whatever we need.

Man must order his brain to accept and conform to the Word. The brain is accustomed to accepting all the garbage that the devil feeds it. Whenever sickness comes, it enters very easily, and becomes manifested in the body. Every time there is a problem, it was because of a defeatist attitude of the brain. Satan had a long time to program us into receiving his junk because we were ignorant.

Now that we know better, we must strengthen ourselves, and act upon the Word. Refuse everything that is not the Word. When you begin to do this, you are going to have a battle. The world, friends, and even your family will come against you. Scripture tells us that we will be persecuted for the Word's sake. When we stand on the Word, we will have opposition, but we cannot be moved by logic. Spirit-filled, born-again believers have to operate well above their present levels in order to bring forth the manifestations of the Word.

Our mission is to bring forth all the knowledge of Jesus Christ. God so loved the world that He sent His Son to save all those who would believe in Him (John

3:16). Bringing the Word to the world seems like an impossible feat, but it's time for us to move out in what the Word says—not trying to understand it, but trusting in God with our complete being. The Word of God is complete, and it will do what it says it will do. God put himself into His Word—His character, personality, promises, plans, purposes, and desires are all found there. God is complete and perfect. He desires His sons and daughters to be manifested like Him.

7

Active Faith and How It Works

Faith is power, and it is an ongoing experience which is always in the present. The Bible speaks of faith as being in the *now.* Faith is active. As soon as believers experience one faith manifestation, they are ready to bring forth the next level of the faith process. The Scripture calls this going from "faith to faith," and from "glory to glory." (See Rom. 1:17 and 2 Cor. 3:18.) It is an ongoing process, and it will progress according to each person's agreement and initiative in fulfilling the Word in their lives. Active faith will lead one into experience, and these experiences will come through the senses. Faith cannot be considered to be complete unless it is experienced through the senses. Hebrews 11:1 states, "Now faith is the substance of things hoped for, the evidence of things not seen." Notice that the Bible says faith is both substance and evidence. Substance and evidence are physical entities, and anything physical must be perceived through the senses. It can be heard, felt, seen, tasted, smelled or experienced.

The world is filled with various types of waves. There are sound waves, microwaves, etc. These waves are produced through vibrations. You cannot see or hear a wave without some kind of receiver. For example, let's say you bring a radio into an empty room and turn it on. Immediately you hear something. It may be someone speaking, or music, or just static. The radio is the receiver for the radio waves. If you turn off the radio, it doesn't mean the radio waves are gone because you can no longer hear them. The radio waves are still there, but the means of receiving them was shut off.

Our brains are the receivers for our souls. The brain receives the signals from our soul. As the brain receives the signals, the body responds. The Word of God will change our hearts. This will cause us to respond, but the emotion is not complete until it is manifested in the body. The brain receives the Word from the soul—the magnificent creation of God—begins to do what it was created to do. Man was created to be in authority on this earth. The first place where authority must be taken by man is over himself. Christians must discipline themselves to obey the Word. We must command our brains to receive the Word in order for it to be manifested in our bodies. The Word that is manifested in and through our bodies will be manifested on this earth, and in this way the glory of God will be manifested also.

In First Peter 3:4, we read about ". . . the hidden man of the heart . . . ." Peter is referring to the inner man. The inner man is a combination of both your soul and your newly created spirit. The body is the vehicle through which the inner man operates. The spirit-man is perfect, and is created in the image and likeness of

God, but the spirit and soul must be in agreement before the body can respond.

In previous chapters, we explained that it was the senses that sinned, and the soul was responsible for the senses. The Bible tells us that we are responsible for our own salvation. God did His job by creating a new creation in us, and now He instructs us by His Word that we are to save our souls through the renewing of our minds. (See Rom. 12:2 and Eph. 4:23.)

In Second Corinthians 4:16, we read that the inward man is being renewed day by day. This is accomplished by bringing the knowledge of the Word into our hearts on a daily basis. This process will make it possible for us to grow into the complete knowledge of God, and to live in His kingdom to the level of our comprehension of the kingdom, on a daily basis.

Matthew 18:19 reads, "Again I say to you that if two of you agree on earth concerning anything that they ask, it will be done for them by My Father in heaven" (NKJV). Let us apply this concept of the power of agreement to *soul and spirit.* The spirit is perfect, but the soul still has the memory of sin that we inherited, a memory that was produced by the flesh. The memory is always there, and the memory, when allowed, will produce its desires. This is why Paul says we must die to our flesh, and this is a daily battle: ". . . the inward man is being renewed *day by day* (2 Cor. 4:16, NKJV, italics mine).

When the soul has been renewed by the Word of God, it will agree with the newly created spirit. This agreement is based on God in both areas—in our spirit through creation, and in our soul through the Word. The newly created spirit is already matured, but the soul is constantly being matured on a daily basis. As the soul matures, it will meet the spirit at that level of maturity, and will receive according to the level of the soul's daily renewal of the mind. Our manifestations will come according to the intensity and application of the Word into our everyday, practical life.

The entire seventh chapter of Romans deals with the battle that rages within the inner man. In verse four of that chapter, the Bible states,

> Therefore, my brethren, you also have become dead to the law through the body of Christ, that you may be married to another—to Him who was raised from the dead, that we should bear fruit to God (Rom. 7:4, NKJV).

This verse deals with the new birth. Paul's telling us that we no longer have any ties to the old being because we have been linked to Jesus, and as Jesus was raised from the dead, we too have been raised from the dead. Our spirits have been born-again.

Paul then goes on to say in verse six, "But now we have been delivered from the law, having died to what we were held by, so that we should serve in the newness of the Spirit and not in the oldness of the letter" (NKJV). Paul is saying that now that we are born-again, we should be serving God from our spirits and not from our minds. The law he is referring to is the law God gave Moses on the mountain.

God gave the people the law so that they could understand that they were doing harm to themselves, and they were sinning against Him. They were spiritually dead unto God because of Adam's sin and had no inner witness or communication with God. God had to communicate to them in the physical realm, and the law was the physical way in which God communicated to them. The body or the flesh was the receiver of what was stored in the heart of man. What man felt was stored up and then sent out as he willed it. "For as he thinketh in his heart, so is he . . ." (Prov. 23:7).

In Jeremiah 24:7, God is speaking to Jeremiah regarding the future generations. He says, "And I will give them an heart to know me, that I am the Lord: and they shall be my people, and I will be their God: for they shall return unto me with their whole heart." Ezekiel 11:19-20 states,

> . . . and I will put a new spirit within you [new creation]; and I will take the stony heart out of their flesh [renewing of their minds—Romans 12:2], and I will give them an heart of flesh. That they may walk in my statutes, and keep mine ordinances, and do them: and they shall be my people, and I will be their God.

God was referring to the New Birth that would manifest on this earth with the sacrifice of Jesus on Calvary. Romans 6:4 records the manifestation of the above two verses as follows: "Therefore we are buried with Him by baptism into death: that like as Christ was raised up from the dead by the glory of the Father, even so we also should walk in newness of life." This newness of life is what Ezekiel 11:19-20 was speaking about.

The heart of man, before the New Birth, is only capable of knowing what he inherited at his natural birth, which is the state of fallen man. Unregenerated, or natural man, is capable of acquiring and perfecting natural knowledge, but he has no understanding of the Word of God. He can be taught morality, decency, order, and obedience, but he is only doing these things out of fear, and most of the time he is frustrated. Because of this frustration he eventually falls into stress, and stress brings sickness to the flesh. Proverbs 28:26 declares that "He that trusteth in his own heart is a fool . . . ." Unless your heart is renewed by the Word of God, you will be doomed to defeat because you were programmed for defeat. God is the only one who can program you to success, and that is done through His Word.

In the seventh chapter of Romans, Paul revealed a struggle he was having with his inner man (soul and spirit). His spirit was telling him what was right, but he wanted to do what his flesh was dictating. Paul was describing a born-again man when he stated:

> For what I am doing, I do not understand. For what I *will* to do, that I do not practice; but what I hate, that I do. If then, I do what I *will* not to do, I agree with the law that it is good. But now, it is no longer I who do it, but sin that dwells in me. For I know that in me (that is, in my flesh) nothing good dwells; for to *will* is present with me, but how to perform what is good I do not find. For the good that I *will* to do, I do not do; but the evil I *will* not to do, that I practice. Now if I do what I will not to do, it is no longer I who do it, but sin that dwells in me [inherent instinct]. I find then a law, that evil is present with me, the one who wills to do good. For I delight in the law of God according to the inward man [soul and spirit]. But I see another

> law in my members, warring against the law of my mind, and bringing me into captivity to the law of sin which is in my members [flesh]. O wretched man that I am! Who will deliver me from this body of death? I thank God—through Jesus Christ our Lord! So then, with the mind I myself serve the law of God, but with the flesh the law of sin (Rom. 7:14-25, NKJV).

In Psalm 8:4, it says, "What is man, that thou art mindful of him? and the son of man, that thou visitest him?" Verse five, states, "For thou hast made him a little lower than the angels, and hast crowned him with glory and honour." The word for angels here is actually *elohim,* meaning "gods." This verse is referring to Genesis 1:26 because verse 6 of Psalm 8 says, "Thou makest him to have dominion over the works of thy hands. Thou has put all things under his feet." David was speaking the words of God over the purpose and direction of man in this world.

In John 10:25, Jesus, speaking to the religious leaders of that time, says, ". . . I told you, and ye believed not: the works that I do in my Father's name, they bear witness of me." The religious leaders asked over and over again who He was, and as religious leaders and masters of the Scriptures, they should have recognized Him, but they didn't. If they would have discerned Genesis 3:15, they would have known that Jesus was the Redeemer. They had a limited understanding of the sacrifice of the blood, and what it really accomplished. They could not see themselves as God had originally created them to be. They did not perceive the purpose of man, which was to have dominion over this earth for the glory of God. They could not see themselves created in the image and after the likeness of God. They began to see themselves in the image the devil was molding for them through the thought process of their minds. For this reason, they always fell back to worshiping idols. This is also the reason why, even to this date, natural man still believes that he evolved from animals. God created man in *His image*, and the devil perverted and distorted the truth by making mankind believe otherwise.

The soul and the spirit are referred to as the inner man, and there is a constant battle going on within that man. The New Creation has the image of God imprinted upon itself, and the soul has the image of natural man imprinted upon itself. Paul is constantly saying that we must be renewed to what the Word says about the New Creation, and, like faith, it must come by hearing, and hearing by the Word of God (Romans 10:17).

Proverbs 16:1 states, "The preparation of the heart belongs to man . . ." (NKJV). God has done His part by the creation of our spirits, and now it is up to us to do our part. In First Peter 1:9, it is written, "Receiving the end of your faith, even the salvation of your souls." Peter refers to "the salvation of your souls," as the responsibility of the believer, but how is this done? In First Peter 1:22, we find the answer, "Seeing ye have purified your souls in obeying the truth through the Spirit unto unfeigned love of the brethren, see that ye love one another with a pure heart fervently." The key part of the verse is "obeying . . . through the spirit." The Spirit of God leads us by guiding our paths. The Spirit of God is the administrator of the Church on the earth. The Father gave us Jesus, and Jesus gave us the Holy Spirit. The Spirit of God is perfect, and will only lead us to perfection.

The Word of God is food for our souls, and is spirit and truth. The Word is knowledge, and as it enters into our hearts it will neutralize the existing knowledge and bring forth the godly activity generated by God's Word. This is what Peter is talking about because he explains it in the same verse. The Word received in our souls, and acted upon, will bring forth love for those we encounter with a pure heart. In other words, we will get results. We will receive what God's Word reveals.

In Hebrews 10:38-39 it says,

> Now the just shall live by faith; but if any man draw back, my soul shall have no pleasure in him. But we are not of them who draw back unto perdition; but of them that believe to the saving of the soul.

Notice that the first part of this verse says, "Now the just shall live by faith." The word "now" is used in Hebrews 11:1. "Now" indicates the present; it involves something going on at the current time. Now is living. Now is being. The just are the ones who are born-again. We have been justified through an act of God, and not on our own accord. Living can also be justified as in the "now" for to be in the "now" you must be living.

Faith is believing in the unseen. Faith is a product of the Word, and the Word produces faith in us. Where is faith produced? It is produced in our soul. My newly created spirit is perfect, and it has the whole Word of God incorporated into it. Our souls have to be saved. The Word is the only way to save our souls. The choice is ours. Man was created with a free will, and he alone must exercise this privilege.

Jesus told us that faith is like a mustard seed (Matthew 17:20). A mustard seed cannot grow unless it's planted. Jesus was giving us a physical explanation of faith by the example of the mustard seed. He was telling us that just as the mustard seed must be planted, so too must our faith be planted. Our faith must be planted in our soul. It must be nourished with the Word, and we must keep on nourishing it on a daily basis. Your faith will grow to the level of your maturity, and to the level of your understanding of your daily personal involvement with the Word. In this growing process, you will be having a battle because what was in your soul before you were born-again will be contrary to what the Word says. The soul area is the battlefield for our daily struggles—the unseen battles that are fought in the now. We have the victory, but it is unseen by the physical eye, and the physical eye only responds to what is being promoted by the soul. Our spirit is our eye to the inner man (spirit and soul). It is the eye to our emotional entity.

". . . Faith comes by hearing . . ." (Rom. 10:17). Faith will come by whatever you hear through your senses. You can receive worldly faith that will hinder and eventually destroy you, or you can receive godly faith, which is produced by the Word, and will bring you great success. This is why it is absolutely imperative that you understand and put into action the entire message of Romans 10:17, ". . . faith cometh by hearing, and hearing by the Word of God." Please take notice of the fact that this verse says "hear*ing*." This indicates implies an ongoing process. You can never get enough of the Word. You must be saturated through and through with the Word of God.

Now that we know that there is a battle, and the victory is already ours, we are told not to draw back—God has no pleasure in anyone drawing back.

The natural is always influencing the human spiritual-sense part of us (our soul). As the Word is being planted in our souls, we are being influenced by our environment, atmosphere and by the circumstances that are controlled by the enemy. Paul confirms this in 2 Corinthians 4:4: "In whom the god of this world hath blinded the minds of them which believe not, lest the light of the glorious gospel of Christ, who is the image of God, should shine unto them." Through this scripture, we see that Satan is referred to as the god of this world. The world that he is referring to is really the age of time, not the physical world. At this time, Satan controls the majority of the human race by his influence over their thoughts, thus causing them to do as he pleases and creating circumstances that are contrary to the Word of God. But we, as born-again believers, are above these circumstances because Jesus has given us the victory. The victory is the Word in our mouths, and it is to be used as a double-edged sword that will change any circumstance that Satan brings against us.

The environmental circumstances that come against us for the Word's sake are instruments the enemy uses to rob the Word from our souls. Mark 4:15-19 gives us an accurate description of what happens when the Word comes into our souls. First, we are told that Satan will come immediately to steal the Word. How does he do this? Because of his influence on this earth, he is able to work through people, places and things by manipulating people's minds with seeds (thoughts) of doubt. Just as the Word will grow and produce faith, doubt too will grow, and it will bring fear. Faith will bring success, and doubt will cause failure. Both faith and doubt are actions that are happening in the now, but cannot be seen with the physical eye. Eventually, however, everything that is in the spiritual will manifest itself in the physical, or in what we commonly call the natural.

Mark 4:16 states that some received the Word with gladness, but they have no root and can only endure for a while, and then they let go. They did not keep hearing and hearing the Word of God. This caused them to become doubtful and to be alienated from God. Watering and feeding can be done only through the Word of God.

The clincher is in Mark 4:19. Here we read that the cares and deceitfulness of this world came in and choked the Word. The god of this age is Satan. He is able to influence the environment to deceive the believer, but he has no authority. He will try to fool you into believing that he does, but this is when the believer must trust in God and see himself as God sees him. He must stand on the promises of God. It is imperative that believers see themselves as God describes them in His Word. The believer has been made in the image, and after the likeness, of God. When he fully understands this, he will become what Mark 4:20 states: "And these are they which are sown on good ground; such as hear the word, and receive it, and bring forth fruit; some thirty-fold, some sixty, and some an hundred."

The seed of the Word grows in the soul, and eventually it will bring forth fruit in the natural realm. The seed is sown in faith in the unseen realm, which then produces fruit or manifestation in the seen realm.

John 15:8 declares, "Herein is my Father glorified, that ye bear much fruit . . . ." God is glorified when we believe on His Word and become saved. His Word is salvation, and when it enters into our dead spirits, we are born-again into a new creation that is created into the image and after the likeness of our Father God (Gen. 1:26). We become just like Him in our spirit-man. Our soul, which is our responsibility (Heb. 10:39), has to be saved. Just as the Word recreated our dead spirit, so too will the Word save our soul.

The soul must be saved in order for the spirit of man to operate through it. Salvation of the soul is accomplished on a continuous basis. As the seed of faith the Word grows in the soul, the fruit of our spirit will manifest more and more through our senses. Salvation of the spirit comes immediately because it is a gift of God. This was done through the sacrifice of Jesus Christ on Calvary, and the only act on our part is to receive it. On the other hand, salvation of the soul is an act of our wills.

The soul is saved in the same way the spirit is saved, and that is through the Word. The Word received into our dead spirit quickens us to a new spiritual life, and the Word received into our soul will change our physical life as well. The soul has to conform to the Word of God, and this can only be done on a personal basis. God cannot intervene in this part of salvation because of our free will. It was the will of man that sinned, and now it is up to the will of man to save his own soul. The saving of the soul is done by applying the Word to it, and not by the works man accomplishes. It is the Word that will bring salvation and success. We must apply the Word to our everyday practical living in the "now," or what is commonly called "the present." Good works will result from this, but it is not good works that save us (James 2:18).

In John 15:7, Jesus says, "If ye abide in me, and my words abide in you, ye shall ask what ye will, and it shall be done unto you." The first part of this Scripture refers to the New Birth. The word "abide" means to be living comfortably and with ease. We could not have Jesus living in us unless we were born-again.

The second part of this verse states, "and my words abide in you." Notice the difference between the first and second part. In the first part Jesus says, "If *ye* abide in me," and this is applying to salvation, but in second part, He says, "and my *words* abide in you." Jesus is now talking about His words. Words are received in the soul area through our senses. Jesus also states that His words must abide in us. The Word must be living comfortably in us, and be so familiar to us that it will be able to guide our every movement. It must penetrate our very existence, and this is done by hearing the Word of God daily.

The first part of this Scripture refers to a new creation, and the second part refers to our soul. Jesus was talking to our inner man. He said that if we lived in Him (salvation), and His words lived in us (renewing of the mind), anything we would ask of the Father would be given to us.

This is very similar to Matthew 18:19, but there is a difference. In John 15:7, it specifically states, ". . . ask what ye will . . ." whereas in Matthew 18:19 it simply states "ask." We don't often see the word "will" put this way, but through this verse, we can see that the will of man is involved in his soul. Because the soul is so corporate and complete, we really cannot segment it into different parts. But in order to get a clearer perspective, we have to attempt to do so.

As we mentioned previously, the soul is the center of our intelligence, emotions and will. Our intelligence is all the accumulated information gathered and received by our senses. Our emotions are formed by the knowledge received through the senses. This knowledge that is received by the senses is transformed into pictures that are stored in our soul (heart). They will eventually become experiences. The more information we receive, the more our emotions will increase until they become a desire. The desire, in turn, will affect our will to perform the action. The will is the power source of man. None of the above can operate alone. All three have to be in operation for any action to be completed—knowledge, desired emotions, and will.

In the process of Christian growth, man will encounter deception, which will cause him to doubt and fail. The power of deception in man's life began in the Garden of Eden. In Genesis 3:5, we hear Satan telling Eve his account of what God said. Now any deception, in order to be believed, must be very much like the truth. His account sounded very good, but it violated a principle, and that principle was obedience. God told Adam and Eve that they were not to touch or partake of the Tree of Knowledge of Good and Evil. Satan came to Eve and began to entice her through deception. He did this by focusing in on why she should eat the fruit. He took her mind off the principle of obedience (Gen. 3:6), and because of this, Eve went immediately from

God's will to her will. It wasn't Satan's will. It was Eve's will. Satan only made the suggestion, but it was Eve who committed the act. She no longer trusted what God said. Instead, she trusted in the knowledge Satan brought to her.

This was the beginning of the sensory—or natural—state of man. Now, man would become dominated by his senses instead of his spirit. Eve had put God in the background and went forward with herself. Now all the knowledge of the devil would be made available to her. She began to see herself as wise (v. 6). Where did she see herself? She saw herself in her imagination, which is part of the soul. Satan's knowledge was received into her soul, which immediately produced the desire, which led to the action. In her imagination, she saw the information she received coming to life, producing an emotion which led to the desire. Then the desire engaged her will to perform the act that led to the downfall of man. Because of this act, to this day we are daily involved in renewing our soul to the original way it was created—to the fullness of the Word of God. Now, when the knowledge of evil comes, we attack it with the Word, producing the image that our Father gave us. This causes us to act "Word-like," which will produce "life abundantly" for ourselves, and it will glorify God.

The Book of Ecclesiastes was written by Solomon, and many Bible scholars believe it was written when he was in a fallen state. He had married foreign women and had gone after their gods. First Kings 11:4 states,

> For it came to pass when Solomon was old, that his wives turned away his heart after other gods, and

> his heart was not perfect with the Lord his God, as was the heart of David his father.

In Ecclesiastes 1:16, we read,

> I communed with mine own heart saying, Lo, I am come to great estate, and have gotten more wisdom than all they that have been before me in Jerusalem: yea, my heart had great experience of wisdom and knowledge.

The words *heart* and *soul* are the same in the Hebrew-Chaldean. Both stem from *nephish.* Notice that Solomon said he had a great experience of knowledge and wisdom in his heart, and then in verse 17 he said, "And I gave my heart to know wisdom, and to know madness and folly: I perceived that this also is vexation of spirit."

When Solomon spoke of this great experience of knowledge and wisdom, he was referring to 1 Kings 3:9 which states,

> Give therefore thy servant an understanding heart to judge thy people, that I may discern between good and bad: for who is able to judge this thy so great a people?

God granted Solomon this request and He supernaturally gifted him with this understanding in his heart (1 Kings 3:12). But now, in Ecclesiastes 1:17, Solomon states that he gave his heart to know wisdom, and also to know madness and folly. In this, he is saying that his heart was once full of the goodness of God, and it was great, and then he became enchanted with the foolishness of men, and this was madness. He goes on to say that it brought a vexation to his spirit. This means that he was troubled in his spirit, and he became confused. He was not able to discern wisdom properly. Godly knowledge and worldly knowledge do not mix. In verse 18 of Ecclesiastes 1, He goes on to say, "For in much wisdom is much grief; and he that increaseth knowledge increaseth sorrow." This statement is the counterpoint of Proverbs 3:13-14, which states, "Happy is the man that findeth wisdom, and the man that getteth understanding. For the merchandise of it is better than the merchandise of silver, and the gain thereof than fine gold."

Solomon was experiencing what Eve had encountered. The Bible tells us that Solomon was the wisest man on earth. He operated for a long period of time in righteousness, but then he began to commune with his own heart, and his heart became full of madness and folly. He was vexed in his spirit because of the battle that was going on inside of him. He gave in to his own self, and fell prey to the deceitfulness of the enemy. This is an accurate example of the battle of the inner man (spirit and soul). He knew what was right, but did what was wrong. The Word is our direct contact with God today. The believer has the same battle in his inner being today, but as long as he keeps the Word inside of him to direct him and guide him, he will be able to overcome. Deception comes into our hearts because of our lack of discretion. Now that we are born-again, we know what is right and what is wrong. What we choose is what we will get. What we are influenced by will dominate our lives. If we are dominated by the Word, we will exemplify the Word and bear good fruit. But if we are affected by the world, we will be in a constant battle; the enemy will be tormenting our minds to cause us grief.

We live in the world—the same world in which Eve and Solomon lived—and the same devil is still here. He is no different. He is still dishing out the same mess. We too can be affected as Solomon was if we allow ourselves to be deceived by what the enemy brings our way. Solomon departed from the Word, and even though he was favored by God, he was doomed by his own actions. Eve also departed from the Word, and she was doomed by her own actions. God doesn't punish us. We walk away from Him and His protection. Because of our free will, we choose our own destiny: blessings, if we choose God (following His Word); or curses, if we depart from His Word.

Psalm 119:69 states, ". . . I will keep thy precepts with my whole heart." Psalm 119:80 echoes this, "Let my heart be sound in thy statutes . . . ." Psalm 119:112 says, "I have inclined mine heart to perform thy statues alway, even unto the end." The word "incline" means "will." Proverbs 6:21 tells us to "Bind them [the Scriptures] continually upon thine heart . . ." and Proverbs 4:4 says to, ". . . Let thine heart retain my words . . . ." Proverbs 4:21 directs, ". . . keep them in the midst of thine heart." Proverbs 4:23 reiterates this important theme, "Keep thy heart with all diligence; for out of it are the issues of life." Proverbs 2:10 tells us, ". . . wisdom entereth into thine heart." When wisdom enters the heart, we can apply our heart to understanding. Understanding is the ability to apply acquired knowledge to cause it to become an action. When all this has been done, "The righteous shall be glad in the Lord, and shall trust in him; and all the upright in heart shall glory" (Ps. 64:10). This puts it all together for us.

Where did Eve and Solomon go wrong? They did not follow Proverbs 3:5-6: "Trust in the Lord with all thine heart; and lean not unto thine own understanding. In all thy ways acknowledge him, and he shall direct thy paths."

Trusting God means to submit completely to the obedience of the Word willingly, regardless of whether we understand it or not. Our understanding will come because of our submission, which is done in faith, and ". . . Faith is the substance of things hoped for, the evidence of things not seen" (Heb. 11:1). The world says that "seeing is believing," but the Word of God says "believing is seeing."

8

The Word–
The Vehicle of God

"Finally, my brethren, be strong in the Lord, and in the power of His might" (Eph. 6:10). How can we be strong in the Lord? Where is God's strength? God tells us that He upholds the world by His Word, so we can be assured that His Word is mighty and powerful. If Jesus is called the "Word" in John 1:14, we can again be equally assured the Lord and the Word are one. Therefore, being strong in the Lord is the same as being strong in the Word. Our strength comes from the Word of God.

> Put on the whole armor of God, that you may be able to stand against the wiles of the devil. For we do not wrestle against flesh and blood, but against principalities, against powers, against the rulers of the darkness of this age, against spiritual hosts of wickedness in the heavenly places (Eph. 6:11-12, NKJV).

We can see by this Scripture that Paul is explicitly telling us that our warfare is not in the physical realm, but in the spiritual realm. He makes this very clear by the phrase, "flesh and blood." Human beings are composed of flesh and blood. Paul is saying that our battle is not against the flesh and blood part of the human being, but against the spirits that are affecting it. Romans 8:1 states, "There is therefore now no condemnation to those who are in Christ Jesus, who do not walk according to the flesh, but according to the Spirit." New-Creation man is created in the image and likeness of God. Real man is a spirit-being like God. He is functioning on this physical earth through his physical body that is made of flesh and blood. This verse tells us to walk according to the Spirit. God and His Word are one. So, we can logically say that the Word and the Spirit are one. To walk according to the Spirit would be the same as to walk according to the Word.

For us to walk or be guided in any way, we must be able to relate to it physically . How can this be done? We can see and hear the Word, but something has to be done with the Word in order for it to "spiritually and physically relate" to us. If our spirit is born-again, it is perfect, and it has the Word in it. Ezekiel 11:19-20 says,

> And I will give them one heart, and I will put a *new* spirit within you, and I will take the stony heart out of their flesh, and I will give them an heart of flesh. That they may walk in mine statutes, and keep my ordinances, and do them, and they shall be my people, and I will be their God.

In our newly created spirit, we walk in the Word of God because God has imprinted His image and likeness into our spirits.

The Word of God is the vehicle through which this happens. It is physical because we can see and hear it, and it is spiritual because it was inspired by God. What makes the Word physical is that we can communicate with it through any of our senses: seeing, hearing, touching, tasting, and speaking. What makes the Word spiritual is the fact that God inspired it. He breathed His Word by way of the pen of man (2 Tim. 3:16). We bring this written Word into our souls through our senses. The Word, which is both spiritual and physical, enters into our minds. When it enters our minds, it becomes spiritual only because we can no longer see or sense it. At this point, the mind decides what it wants to do with it. The unrenewed mind is at enmity with the Word and therefore wants to reject it (Rom. 8:7), but the renewed mind will receive it. From the mind, the Word will enter our hearts where it will build up in picture form. The more of the Word that we receive, the stronger the image becomes. The Word must operate in the unseen realm, which we call the spiritual realm, before it becomes manifested in the physical realm. Our confidence (faith) is constantly being built up through the abundance of the Word that is being processed through our hearts. The reality of the Word eventually causes us to act on this confidence, and it will come out as an action. This action is the manifestation of the Word. The spiritual becomes physical. You may either speak it out or act it out, and then apply it to whatever need or desire you may have. This is summed up in Hebrews 11:1, ". . . Faith is the substance of things hoped for, the evidence of things not seen."

Here's an example. The Bible tells us that by the stripes of Jesus we have been made whole (1 Pet. 2:24). This gives us the right to walk in divine health. Our bodies have the ability to reject sickness, and now because we are saved, we have the legal right to this ability because Jesus took away all our sickness, griefs and infirmities (Isa. 53:3-5).

But one day you wake up and you feel sick, and your body begins to receive infirmity. Simultaneously, the Word begins to rise up in your heart where you have been depositing it. You begin to speak to the infirmity, and you tell it that it has no right to invade your body. The more you speak the Word over the infirmity, the more confidence you build up. Your mind will give you a struggle because it wants to acknowledge the sickness, but keep on denying the right for it to be there. The more that you speak the physical Word (sense), the more it will increase spiritually (unseen) in your soul. Eventually, this becomes a strong emotional feeling, and this feeling will burst forth into an action of faith that causes the sickness to leave your body.

You will become what you have received. What you have received was the Word of God, and the Word became manifested in you. Healing is your right. The Word carries healing, and it was expressed in you. The Word became alive through your actions, and it manifested the healing. The healing received was a process of the Word within you, a process that was both physical and spiritual. It entered into the soul where it took on the nature of the soul (which is spiritual), and received it in the body as healing.

In order to walk in the Word, you must know who you are and what you are. Let's begin with who you are in Christ. You are the redeemed of the Lord. You were redeemed by the blood of Jesus, and you were made righteous by His sacrifice on Calvary. What you are in Christ comes from what He gained for you. Jesus became your substitute. He became the substitute for unregenerated man, and He took our fallen nature and nailed it to the cross. It was finished once and for all as He uttered the words, *It is finished.* Man was now able to be in the position to receive, as a rightful heir, his inheritance in the Kingdom of God. If there is sickness in your life, it has no right to be there. If there is lack in your life, it has no right to be there. Deny the right for any curses to be on any born-again child of God. What you received must agree with Whom you've received. Jesus is complete in every way, and if you have received Him, you are complete and should be operating in that completion. You identify with Him positionally because of who you are *in* Him, and you identify in what you are by what you receive from Him. The *substance* of faith is your *evidence.* The answer to sickness is healing. The answer to lack is prosperity. Our legal right to healing and prosperity was given to us by God, but we must take this right and apply it to the areas of our life that need it.

> This book of the law shall not depart out of thy mouth; but thou shalt meditate therein day and night, that thou mayest observe to do according to all that is written therein: for then thou shalt make thy way prosperous, and then thou shalt have good success (Josh. 1:8).

This is the complete principle for success. Let's examine this Scripture closely. Remember, we are now engaged in the area of "walking in the Word," or what may be more commonly called "living the Word." God's Word is conditional. If you do what He says, then you will receive what He has promised. This is called the "if and then principle." The first part of this Scripture, "This book of the law shall not depart out of thy mouth . . ." may be considered to be a commandment. This is the first part, the *if.* The last part of this verse continues with the *then,* "and then thou shalt have good success." Success is the result of the *if,* and it is the completion of the *then.*

Our text verse is a statement that contains a condition—the condition is that if we obey, we will receive. If we keep the Word in our mouths, we will have good success. Because we were created in the image and after the likeness of God, we have a free will just like God, and He always gives us a choice to make with a condition attached. He wants us to exercise our free wills. The will of man is his power source, and man cannot do anything unless his will is involved.

God even tells us the results of our choices, yet He leaves it up to us to make the decisions. He told Adam and Eve not to eat of the Tree of the Knowledge of Good and Evil. He also told them what would happen if they did eat the fruit, but He did not force them or inhibit them in any way. He gave them all the facts and the answers, but it was up to them to decide for themselves. At that time, they were endowed with the glory and wisdom of God, and they knew only good. They had no idea of what evil was. It wasn't necessary for them to know evil because good always overcomes evil. But when they partook of the Tree of the Knowledge of Good and Evil, they were confronted with evil for the first time. From then on they were involved with both good and evil, and this forced them to make a decision before every action. Because of their decision, everything we encounter, requires us to examine the pros (good) and the cons (evil) before making a choice. Because of their fall, we will always be plagued with this burden.

But God had His solution ready even before our original parents fell and created the problem for us. In His Word we have the complete directions of where we are to go and what we are to do. If we obey His Word in keeping with the *if* and *then* principle, we will receive all that He has promised to us in His Word.

Not only does God give us the answer to each condition, but He tells us how to do it. In Joshua 1:8, He tells us to, ". . . meditate therein day and night." The word "meditate" comes from the Hebrew-Chaldean word *hagah,* which means to murmur, to ponder, imagine, mutter, roar, speak, study, talk, utter. This definition is completely self-explanatory. If you really want to remember something, you will always begin by murmuring it to yourself, and you will do this over and over again. If it is important enough, you will ponder it until you have developed it into picture form in your imagination. Now that it is in picture form, you can mutter it at will, or roar it in confidence. When you are confident of something, you will not hesitate to speak, and the more that it is discussed, the more you will want to know. So you study, and the more that you study, the more you will talk about it. In order to remember what you studied, you will constantly be uttering it. This is the basic principle for learning anything in life, and it starts at a very early age.

From your child's infancy, put this principle into practice. When you introduce something new to him, he will fix his eyes upon it, often staring at the article for a long time. This is the observation stage. After he has observed it for a while, he begins to make audible sounds as if he were speaking. The more familiar he becomes with the object, the more excited he becomes. He may even begin to scream or roar. As you continue to observe him, he will pick up the object and begin to study it all over again, trying to find some new interesting aspect of it. Not finding anything new or different at this time, he may cast it aside. But upon picking up the article or toy at a latter time, he will become once more excited because he sees something familiar, and he will go through the same routine as before; observing, meditating (studying), and doing.

If you do the meditating successfully, it will become natural to you. The degree of your success will depend on the amount of meditation that you do. If you are obedient to the Word, you will meditate on the Word day and night. This does not mean that you literally have to be reading the Bible day and night, but it does mean that you have to apply the Word to whatever you do as you are doing it.

This is the reason why you must go to church and sit under an anointed pastor who preaches the uncompromised Word. This is the reason why you must enroll in all the classes that are made available to you, and pursue more and more knowledge that can be turned into wisdom. Joshua 1:8 ends with, "and then thou shalt have good success." The world has used this principle over and over again, and by so doing many have had success in whatever they have done. God's success is guaranteed. He is Jehovah who teaches us to profit.

Isaiah 48:17, "I am the Lord thy God which teacheth thee to profit, which leadeth thee by the way that thou shouldest go." The world (unbelievers) does not have this guarantee or right. We, as believers, should be so well-versed in the Word that when a difficult circumstance comes up, we are immediately prepared to combat it with the Word. It is the Word that will bring us to where we belong, and that is in complete authority over all of the earth.

Because authority is given to a person, it doesn't always mean that he will take it. Real biblical authority is received through submission. In Matthew 8:9 and Luke 7:8, there is the account of the Roman centurion who came to Jesus and requested Him to heal his servant. When Jesus told him that He would come to heal his servant, the centurion replied that it wasn't necessary for Him to come, but all that He had to do was speak a word, and his servant would be healed. He said to Jesus, "For I am a man under authority, having soldiers under me. . . ." Being under authority is the same as being submissive to authority, and because of his submission, he was placed in authority over men. The centurion understood both the value of submission and the power of authority. The difference for us to note is that *spiritual authority cannot be earned—it must be received and exercised.* If you do not exercise authority, it will remain dormant and you will lose it because it is not evident.

It is our submission to Jesus as the Lord of our lives that gives us the right to act on His behalf. We submit to Him, and He reinstates the authority that was given to man in the Garden. Along with this authority comes the image of God. We must have an image in order to exercise authority. A policeman bases his authority upon the legislation that allows him to act in his authority, but it is his uniform that enables us to recognize that authority. His uniform becomes an image that represents his authority. His confidence is built up because of that image, and he acts from this confidence by projecting the authority that has been given to him. ". . . and I say to this man, go and he goeth . . ." (Matt. 8:9).

Imagination plays a tremendous part in a person assuming his authority. In Joshua 1:8 we are told to meditate on the Word day and night. One of the words used to define meditation is "to imagine." Words form images, and images become life-like and are stored in our hearts (subconscious). These images are what we act out in life. In order for us to apply our God-given authority, we must see ourselves as God has created us. In Matthew 17:2 and Mark 9:2, we have the account of Jesus' transfiguration on the mountain. Jesus took Peter, James and John up to the mountain where He was transfigured in front of them. This transfiguration was for the benefit of mankind. It was a type and shadow of the born-again experience. Believers, for the very first time, would see who they were as born-again sons of God.

To understand the transfiguration, we must understand God and His Word. His Word reveals to us that He gave man all authority on this earth. So God cannot (because

He is bound to His Word) directly act on this earth. He has to operate through man. Although Jesus is God, He operated on this earth entirely as man endowed with the Holy Spirit. When Jesus was transfigured on the mountain, He was showing mankind who He was. The Bible says, ". . . and his face did shine as the sun, and His raiment was white as the light" (Matt. 17:2). Everything that happened to Jesus on this earth, He experienced as a man. He was our example of what we would become. Jesus was showing us our image, the image of God inside of us. Jesus was showing His disciples their heavenly status by the example of Him talking with Moses and Elijah, and their earthly status by letting them see this experience as it happened in His physical being. Jesus revealed himself to be the complete man that He is—a spirit with a soul, living in a body.

The disciples did not know what was happening at the time. Peter began to ask questions about building tents for Jesus, Moses and Elijah, and a very interesting thing happened. A cloud appeared over them, and God the Father said, ". . . This is my beloved Son, in whom I am well pleased; hear ye him" (Matt. 17:5). God was showing mankind, through Jesus, that they too would be as Jesus. We would become sons of God through the sacrifice of Jesus.

The sixteenth chapter of Matthew gives the full account of Jesus telling His disciples about His need to go to Jerusalem to lay down His life for man. This is where Jesus asked them,

> . . . Whom do men say that I, the Son of man, am? And they said, Some say that thou art John the Baptist;

> some, Elias; and others, Jeremias, or one of the prophets. He saith unto them, But whom say ye that I am? And Simon Peter answered and said, Thou art the Christ, the Son of the living God (Matt. 16:13-16).

Peter answered boldly because he was operating from the promised born-again nature by faith. The Spirit of God revealed to him the deity of God in Jesus. This is why Jesus said to Peter, "Blessed art thou, Simon Barjonah: for flesh and blood hath not revealed it unto thee, but my Father which is in heaven" (Matt. 16:17). Peter was speaking from the born-again nature that would be physically manifested upon the death and resurrection of Jesus Christ.

In Matthew 16:18, Jesus said to Peter, "Thou art Peter, and upon this rock, I will build my church." Jesus was speaking to mankind. Peter was the representation of man with the born-again nature. The rock that Jesus was speaking about was himself. In Psalms 118:22-23 we read, "The stone which the builders refused is become the head stone of the corner. This is the Lord's doing; it is marvellous in our eyes." Isaiah 28:16 tells us more:

> Therefore thus saith the Lord God, Behold, I lay in Zion for a foundation a stone, a tried stone, a precious corner stone, a sure foundation: he that believeth shall not make haste.

And to sum it all up, Jesus said,

> Did ye ever read in the scriptures, The stone which the builders rejected, the same is become the head of

> the corner: this is the Lord's doing, and it is marvellous in our eyes? (Matt. 21:42).

We can be well assured that Peter was not the rock because he did not fit the qualifications. The church would be built upon the Word of God which is the same as the rock, Jesus Christ. (See John 1:14, "And the Word was made flesh . . . .")

The remainder of Matthew 16:18 states, "and the gates of hell shall not prevail against it." In the next verse, Jesus tells Peter why: "I will give unto thee the keys of the kingdom . . . ." Jesus is speaking directly to Peter, but indirectly He is speaking to all of us because Peter here represents born-again mankind.

What are the keys of the kingdom? The keys to the kingdom are found in God's Word. If born-again man is in authority, where did his authority come from? He received this authority from the mouth of God through His Word (Gen. 1:26). That Word, spoken in the Garden of Eden is accomplishing that which it was sent for. Psalm 119:160 verifies this: "Thy word is true from the beginning: and every one of thy righteous judgments endureth for ever." Hebrews 1:3 expresses the power of God's Word: "Who being the brightness of His glory, and the express image of His person, and upholding all things by the word of his power . . . ." God is telling us that He puts His Word over His power. His power is so awesome that mere words cannot be found to explain it, and God is telling us that His Word is even more significant than His power. God has given born-again, Spirit-filled, man His Word to use on this earth. Jesus confirms this in Matthew 16:19 where He states, "whatsoever thou shalt bind on earth shall be bound in heaven: and whatsoever thou shall loose on earth shall be loosed in heaven." Jesus told us where the keys are, and then told us to go ahead and use them. The entire Kingdom of God is governed by His Word which always remains the same because Jesus is the same yesterday, today, and forever (Heb. 13:8).

In reading Matthew 16, we can now understand why Jesus took Peter, James and John with Him to the mountain. He wanted them to see with their own eyes what He was teaching them. He was showing them what He wanted them to know instead of just instructing them. Jesus was telling them that they would be given the keys, and they would have the authority to use them. Up to that point, however, they had no concept of what Jesus was conveying to them. So Jesus took them to the mountain, and gave them a glimpse of themselves through His Transfiguration—the renewed spirit of man, with the Holy Spirit residing and reigning in him.

Matthew 17:2 says that His face shone as bright as the sun. This was the glory of God, and this same Glory is in us. God was showing us what Genesis 1:26 states. We are made in the image and after the likeness of Him. We are to take this example from the Scriptures and meditate on it until it becomes so impressed in our imagination, so strong that we see ourselves in the same manner as God sees us—doing the same things that Jesus did on a regular basis. He fed the thousands, healed all the sick of their infirmities, raised the dead and walked on water. Nothing was impossible for Him. He knew who He was.

Do you know who you are? Are you doing what

Jesus did? If not, then keep on reading His accounts, and remember that we can do the same things He did because He said that we could. "He that believeth on me, the works that I do shall he do also" (John 14:12). Cultivate daily the image of God in you. See the transfiguration of the New Creation in you, in your imagination. See yourself laying hands on the sick, and the sick recovering. See yourself prospering so you can further the Kingdom of God. Remember there is only one God, and He reigns in *you*, within your newly created spirit, and He wants to and will manifest His Word through you—if you will allow Him to.